To Marry, Go

on

/ Cor 13

Bill Kyne

Love
That Lasts a
Lifetime

Love
That Lasts a
Lifetime

BILL KYNE

ARCHWAY PUBLISHING

Archway Publishing books may be ordered through booksellers or by contacting:

Archway Publishing
1663 Liberty Drive
Bloomington, IN 47403
www.archwaypublishing.com
1 (888) 242-5904

Because of the dynamic nature of the Internet, any web addresses or links contained in this book may have changed since publication and may no longer be valid. The views expressed in this work are solely those of the author and do not necessarily reflect the views of the publisher, and the publisher hereby disclaims any responsibility for them.

Any people depicted in stock imagery provided by Getty Images are models, and such images are being used for illustrative purposes only. Certain stock imagery © Getty Images.

This book is a work of non-fiction. Unless otherwise noted, the author and the publisher make no explicit guarantees as to the accuracy of the information contained in this book and in some cases, names of people and places have been altered to protect their privacy.

ISBN: 978-1-4808-6356-9 (sc)
ISBN: 978-1-4808-6357-6 (hc)
ISBN: 978-1-4808-6358-3 (e)

Library of Congress Control Number: 2018949014

Print information available on the last page.

Archway Publishing rev. date: 6/28/2018

Contents

Introduction

Love

MOST PEOPLE GO THROUGH LIFE SEARCHING for, hoping for, and praying for love—true love. It's that once in a lifetime kind of love—the kind of love you read about in books, poems, or trashy novels. It's the kind of love you hear about in thousands of love songs written about it and the kind you see on TV or in the hundreds of movies that are made about it.

Love

It makes the world go around.

Love

It's all you need according to the old Beatles song.

Love

Poets, writers, filmmakers, songwriters, and TV producers keep our hopes and dreams alive by writing about, singing about, and showing us all about this thing called love.

Love

Do you want to find love? Have you ever found love? I mean *true* love. Do you believe it really exists? Do you believe there is a true love out there for everyone? Do you think there's only one true love for each of us? Does it only come along once in a lifetime? What happens if you miss it? Is that all there is for you? Do you have to settle for whatever else you can get?

Love

It's such a powerful word. There has been more written about love than just about anything else in the world. After all, isn't that what most of us want more than anything else? It's that awesome feeling you get when you meet that special someone and they consume your every thought, hope, emotion, and desire. You can gain all the wealth in the world, and you can go after all the fame you can imagine. You can even seek to be completely spiritual, but what would it be without...

Love!

Most people would love to experience it once in a lifetime—true love. The kind of love you read about in books like Shakespeare's *Romeo and Juliet*. The kind of love you hear about and feel in all those love songs like "Feels So Right" by Alabama. It's the kind of love you see in movies like *Titanic*.

How many people really get to experience that kind of love? Evidently some have. Otherwise those songs, stories, and movies wouldn't be so popular. They keep the hope and dream alive by romanticizing this crazy thing called...

Love!

Paul McCartney wrote a song that says "Some people want to fill the world with silly love songs... And what's wrong with that?"

Have you ever had true love in your life? Do you want to have it? Do you believe it's even really out there? Or has it been just an illusion, something you've just read about, heard in a song, or seen in a movie?

Love

Through the curse of my life, I have had the pleasure of knowing true love. I know it exists. I've had it happen to me. I've experienced it, and it can be awesome! I know for a fact it's out there. You have to be open to it. It may come when you least expect it. It may come when you're not looking. Then again, it could come while you are looking and are ready. Who knows what the right time is for you?

This book is about my experiences with this ever-elusive thing called love. I've had the opportunity to live it. I have had the distinct pleasure of finding that special kind of love that all those songs, movies, and poems are written about. This is the story of my life from the beginning of how I found love (or how love found me) to the present and everything in between.

Yes, I have found true love. I've also lost it. That special kind of love is fabulous while it's there—while you're in it. You feel like you're on top of the world, and you never want it to end. It makes it all the more devastating when you lose it. Still, even though I lost it, I wouldn't have missed it for anything in the world.

Garth Brooks wrote a song called "The Dance." It talks about that type of thing. If you could know then what you know now, would you still go through with it? Would you still risk the hurt you feel at the end for the feelings you get while you are in that moment? *Yes!* I would anyway. I would because to not go through it, to not experience the love and the pain, you would have to miss "The Dance."

This book is about life, love, living, and dying. It's about the ups and downs of love and life. Sometimes it seems that life is not fair. You may feel you got the short end of the stick. Other times you may feel like life is wonderful and that you're on top of the world! In my opinion, the great times far outweigh the bad… if *you* let them. A lot of how your life and love turn out is up to you. You are the one who gets to decide how you feel about the things that happen to you. It can take work and effort sometimes to make love—true love—real and worth having. After all, you get out of this life and love what you put in to it. It is well worth the effort though. Nothing I know of can bring you greater joy than *true love.*

Now, let me tell you my story of ***Love That Lasts A Lifetime***

Chapter 1

From the Beginning

TO UNDERSTAND AND SEE THAT EVEN YOU can find true love, you have to know that if it happened to me, it can happen to anyone. Let me just start from the beginning.

When I was growing up, I had pretty good role models for how marriage should be. My mom and dad seemed happy and stayed married. On both sides of my family, my grandparents were married all their lives and seemed happy. My grandparents laughed and joked with each other, showed affection, and kissed once in a while. So did my mom and dad. Sure, there were ups and downs, but for the most part, they all showed me what these things called love and marriage were all about. At least it seemed that way to me. To me and for a lot of other people who grew up in my day and age, that was the American dream. You grew up, found a girl (or a guy), got married, bought a house, and raised a family together. A little kissing and hugging, a vacation to the lake or to the beach once in a while, and you were set. That was the way I thought life was supposed to be. Ah, but what did I know? I was only a kid.

I was always kind of an adventurous young man. We lived up north in Pennsylvania and Connecticut until I was in the sixth grade, and then our family moved to Florida. Being adventurous, I was always looking for some type of thrill. I learned to ride a motorcycle when I was thirteen—and I loved it! My brother and I would go off in the summer and venture into the woods, creeks, and bayous around the Tampa Bay area; we would head out there with a patched-together boat, fishing gear, a knife, and matches, and we would just live off the land for about a week at a time. We would do things like jump off bridges, swim in the creek, and fish in the Gulf of Mexico.

When I was in high school, I played sports and was on the football team. Being athletic and one of the bigger guys on the team, I played on the defensive line. I was always pretty competitive, and I excelled at team sports. I had been working at one job or another from a very early age. Even at that time in my life, I liked being independent and having my own money.

While I was in high school, I got a job at a gas station that was owned by a biker who my dad knew. They both frequented the same bar, which was right down the street from where we lived. My dad would stop there after work, and I would go hang out there with him sometimes. I got to meet some of the other bikers, shooting pool with them and hearing some of their stories. They would always talk about going on a run or coming back from another run from Miami or going to Daytona Bike Week. They always had lots of money and lots of girls hanging around with them. I thought their lifestyle was great, so when Jerry offered me a job as a station attendant at his garage, I jumped at the chance. My high school days were numbered from then on.

I had my own bike—not a Harley like theirs, but still a bike. The more I hung around with them, the less I was into school and sports. And before you knew it, I was skipping school to hang with them. It wasn't long after that when I quit school completely in the middle of my senior year. That was real smart, huh? Then I started with the drinking, and before long I got into drugs. After all, that's what they were doing, and they were "cool." I wanted to be cool, so I tried doing what they did. I started running errands for them, carrying packages from a car lot they ran to a place in Miami. Sometimes they would allow me to go on rides with them. I was kind of like their big pet. They would tell me to do something, and I would do it. Once in a while they had me pick fights with guys for no reason, just to see if I would do it. I wanted to be cool and to fit in, so I did it. Most of the time I won, and when it looked like I was in trouble, they would jump in and bail me out. I thought that was the life. Plenty of money, plenty of women, and plenty of drugs and alcohol. I wasn't even old enough to drink legally yet, but because I was with them, I was always served at any bar we went to. Sex, drugs, and rock and roll. *What could be better?* I thought. *Just what every growing boy needs to become a man!*

Quitting high school wasn't the brightest move—and I knew it—so I did go back to vocational school to learn to be an auto mechanic. I wanted to learn to work on my own cars and bikes, which I was doing to some extent but wanted to learn the right way. I also wound up getting a part-time job as a bouncer at a club called Park Lounge in Pinellas Park. It was a very rough club, and they would average two or three fights a night on weekends. They had a hard time keeping bouncers because of all the fights. I used to hang out there anyway, so when they asked if I would take the job and told me it paid an hourly wage *and* free drinks, I said, "Heck yes!" I figured just the free drinks would be saving me a lot of money. I still wasn't old enough to drink legally, but they didn't need to know that.

Back then I thought fighting was fun, and I got good at it. I developed the reputation of a guy who didn't take any crap from anyone, and if you started a fight at the lounge, I would finish it. By the second month of working at the bar, the fights were down to one or two a weekend—and the owner was happy. I was also going to school full time, and then I got a job as a mechanic at a garage as well.

Between school, my job as a mechanic, and my job at the lounge—
and my social life with the bikers—things were very busy. A typical
weekend would start Friday morning with me being at school by seven
thirty in the morning. I would get off at noon and be at the garage by
twelve thirty. There I would work until eight and then go home and get
cleaned up and head to the lounge by nine. I would work there until two
in the morning, and then I would head to the bottle club until six or
seven. That was the place where all the people who worked in the bars
hung out after hours, drinking and doing whatever else happened to be
going on. My life was getting out of control. I was still running packages,
still partying like a rock star, still doing drugs, and still drinking. Then
I would get out and do stupid stunts on my bike, like riding a wheelie
down the road, jumping a twenty-five-foot ditch on a street bike, or
racing police cars. Yeah, it was stupid stuff.

When I was drunk or high (often both), I thought I was ten feet
tall and bulletproof. My friends and family all told me I would probably
be either dead or in prison before I was twenty-one. The crowd I was
running with, the lifestyle I was leading, and the job I had were driving
me down a path of self-destruction.

As for me, I thought I was living the dream. I was drinking before
I was legal; I had plenty of drugs, girls, and money; and I was about to
graduate from auto-repair school. What more could a growing boy need?
The last thing I thought I would ever want or need was a relationship. It
was like the scene with Joe Pesci in the movie *Goodfellas* when his mom
said, "You need to settle down with a good girl." And his response was,
"I settle down with a girl almost every night. Difference is I leave in the
morning."So when a friend of mine from the garage I was working at
suggested that I take this good girl who was his neighbor out on a date,
I said, "No way. I don't have the time, and I don't want to."

He kept after me though. I would sometimes have dinner with him
and his wife. They were not part of the crowd I ran with. Wayne was a

family man and a Christian. I enjoyed their company though, and his wife, Carroll, was a good cook, so that was a plus. She would often bring Wayne dinner at the shop, and she would always make sure there was enough for both of us. Once in a while Wayne and I would go fishing after work during the week. They both kept on about taking out their neighbor. I asked, "What does she look like?" Typical guy, right?

Carroll said, "Well, her name is Kris and she is very slender and good-looking and fun to be with. Oh, and she has two kids."

I said, "What? No way! I'm not getting involved with a lady who already has two kids!"

They told me she had been through a tough time and was living back at home. They wanted someone to show her a nice time for her birthday, which was coming up. They asked me to at least think about it. I told them I would think about it but that I probably wasn't going to do it.

Wayne got to know me a bit and saw the crowd I was running with and the lifestyle I was leading. He heard some of the stories of things that were going on at the bar, the club, and the bike runs. He told Carroll about it, and she said, "I know, but I see a nice guy under that tough-guy image he's trying to put on. He's not that guy when he's around us."

They kept on, and I finally said, "I'll tell you what. I will come over and meet her. We'll see where it goes from there." I just said that to get them to stop harping on me about it. They were excited and set up a meeting.

One night after work I'd told Wayne and Carrol I would drop by. I rushed home, took a quick shower, and headed to their place. They lived in an upstairs apartment behind Kris's parents' house. She had been out back cleaning the yard for hours and was sweeping up when I got there. I was riding my bike and had long, wet hair that probably looked like it was greasy, so I was a mess myself. Neither of us was impressed with what we saw.

There I was, a big biker with long, wet hair, and she was wearing a plaid shirt and shorts with messy hair and had been cleaning the yard all day. I came to find out later that she didn't even know she was going to meet me that night. She thought I was coming over to go fishing with Wayne.

Carroll introduced us and said, "This is Bill, the guy who works with Wayne. He's going to take you out for your birthday next week."

Talk about putting us both on the spot! There we were. We had just met, and neither one of us was impressed with the other. Now we were going out on a date that neither of us wanted in the first place! I thought to myself, *Thanks a lot, Carroll. I'll get you back for this!* On the outside I said "Oh, okay, what time should I pick you up?" We talked for a few minutes and made plans for me to pick her up the following Wednesday at seven. We would be celebrating her birthday and my graduation from auto repair school the same day—August 6, 1976. It was the day Kris turned twenty-one and the day I graduated from Pinellas Vocational Technical Institute. I was nineteen at the time, still wild and crazy, still running with a much older crowd.

The girls I'd been dating at the time were usually much older too–biker chicks, bar maids, topless dancers—women like that. Like I said, I was a *long* way from settling down. I figured I would go out with Kris one time as a favor to Wayne and Carroll, and that would be it. Kris could get back to her life, and I could get back to mine. Or so I thought… I was definitely *not* looking for love.

Sometimes love has to find you!

Chapter 2

The First Date

THE FOLLOWING WEDNESDAY, I'D MADE plans to take Kris out for dinner. As I said it was her birthday, and because I'd just graduated from automotive repair school as well I was in a celebrating mood. To me that meant going out and getting wasted and partying with friends at the bar. Since I had a date with Kris the getting wasted and partying would come later. I was planning on getting together with some friends after our date and really celebrating.

I got ready for the evening and put on my best blue jeans and my best biker boots. I did up my long, bushy hair and put on some cologne and a loud, flowery dress shirt. It was a deep blue with large orange and white flowers on it. If you were around in the '70s, you know the kind of shirt I'm talking about. After getting ready, I got on my bike and rode down to pick up Kris. I figured she would be dressed in jeans too or at least in pants. After all, she knew that we were going out on my bike, right? That's what I thought anyway.

Actually, we'd never discussed it. She'd told me that she'd never been on a bike before. She didn't know anything about riding. I never mentioned the fact that it was the only transportation I had. All she knew was that I was taking her out to a nice restaurant that evening. She said she liked seafood, so I told her I would choose the place and take care of everything. To me that meant making reservations and paying the bill. Oh, and showing up on time. After all, I could be a gentleman sometimes.

When I got to her house, I parked the bike on the street in front of her house and went to the door. After I rang the doorbell, Kris opened the door and was standing there wearing a long evening gown and high heels. Her makeup was done just right, and she looked very elegant. *Wow!* She was drop-dead gorgeous! Talk about making a good second impression! She was stunning! I felt stupid and *way* underdressed for the evening. There I was with long, bushy hair in jeans with a loud flowered shirt on a motorcycle. At least it was a dress shirt and my boots were shined.

She looked at me and smiled. Then she looked out and saw my bike and looked back at me with a concerned look on her face. I just stood there dumbfounded and started to say something and it just came out as, "Ahh, I don't... ahh... I'm not, ahh. I thought, aah."

Just then Kris's dad, Hoyt, came up and introduced himself. I looked him in the eyes and shook his hand and introduced myself to him.

He looked at me, then looked out at my bike and said, "You're not planning on taking my daughter out on *that* thing, are you?"

I said, "Well, sir, that's all I have. I don't own a car."

He then looked at his daughter, looked back at me, went into his pocket, and handed me the keys to his car. He said, "Take care of my daughter."

I was shocked and said "Yes, sir, I sure will, and I'll take good care of your car too. Thank you very much."

Now, to appreciate how bizarre that was you would have to know Kris's dad, Hoyt. He had four daughters and didn't like *anybody* who dated or even married his daughters. To tell the truth, he didn't like people that much either. He was born and raised in Alabama and spent most of his life in northern Alabama and Georgia up in the hills, small towns, and backwoods. He even ran moonshine when he was younger, I learned later. He was a pure country redneck.

He was very protective of his daughters—too protective, they would say. He was the kind of guy who would meet his daughters/ dates at the door with a loaded gun or sharpening a knife. One time the youngest sister, Yvette, had a date, and Hoyt met him at the door. He said to him, "I hear you're a pretty smart young fella. Can you read between the lines?" The guy just looked at him kinda bewildered, and Hoyt said, "Well, read this." He opened his hand and there were six bullets in it. The gun was implied.

So when he met me there at the door, looking like I did and riding what I rode, for him to offer me his car to take his daughter out was like Moses parting the Red Sea!

We went to dinner, and I tried to be a perfect gentleman. I opened her door for her and pulled out her chair at the restaurant.

I treated her the way a lady should be treated. I knew *how* to do that kind of stuff. My momma raised me right. I just didn't do it very often. With the type of girls I was seeing, being a gentleman wasn't necessary. That night with Kris looking the way she did, I wanted to make a good second impression myself.

We had a good dinner and a great time. I even refrained from drinking, something that was rare for me back then. We found that we were very comfortable talking with each other and got along great. Actually, at first I did most of the talking. I told her quite a bit about myself—the good stuff anyway. I did seem to omit a lot of the things I was doing and how I was living at that time. I was talking mostly in generalizations and about my automotive trade school, about high school and my work at the garage. I told her how Wayne and I met and about how we would go fishing sometimes after work. She told me she enjoyed fishing herself and used to go with her dad sometimes.

To get Kris to open up, I had to prod just a bit. She was very guarded. She had been hurt in relationships before, and I could see that. I was patient and encouraged her to tell me about her life, and then I listened. That was a novel thing for me to do at the time. With Kris it was easy, though, and I found myself genuinely interested in her and what she had to say. To this day I don't remember everything we talked about. However, I do remember looking into her eyes and being intrigued by the lovely young lady who was sitting across from me. We talked for quite a while and had a great dinner. We really enjoyed each other's company.

I drove her home and walked her to the door of her house and kissed her goodnight. Then I went in with her to thank her dad and give him back his car keys. Hoyt was sitting there in his chair watching TV. I handed him his keys, shook his hand, and thanked him again for his generosity with his car. I told him I would be better prepared the next time.

He said, "So there's going to be a next time?"

I looked at Kris and said, "Well, it's up to her, but I certainly hope so."

She just smiled at me and said, "I think I'd like that."

She then walked me out to my bike, and I got ready to leave. We kissed again and started talking. I never did make it out to celebrate with my friends that night. Instead we sat outside her house talking for over an hour before I got on the bike and rode home.

Instead of going out partying that night, I went home and just thought about the night's events. I said to myself, "Wow, she was really nice and easy to talk to. Not to mention how *hot* she was in that dress!" I even found myself wondering about her kids and how it would be to hang out with them around. She had told me a little bit about them (after a bit of prodding) at dinner. As I said, she was pretty guarded and didn't open up a whole lot about them.

I went to bed that night and tried not to think about her anymore. The night was over, and the favor was done. I would get back to my life, and she could get back to hers. I could get Wayne and Carroll off my back and I didn't need to hear any more about it from them. That should be it, right? There was only one problem with that train of thought. There was just one thing that was stopping that from happening—one thing stopping me from just going back to the way my life was before and that was... *Kris!*

As I said in the beginning, love comes sometimes when you least expect it, when you're not looking for it, and sometimes when you don't even *want* it!

Love can be sneaky and can come when you least expect it.

Chapter 3

Getting to Know Her

WHEN LOVE COMES ALONG, IT CAN CHANGE things. It can change the way you think, the way you see things, the things you tend to hear, and sometimes the very way you live. At the time I had my first date with Kris, I was seeing other girls. By the time our third date came around, I was only seeing Kris. We would do things like go to the movies and go out to dinner. Then we would just talk and have a good time enjoying getting to know one another. It was a totally different experience for me—going on an actual date and not just to some bar or a party, getting wasted, and trying to remember the next morning who I was with and what went on the night before.

Kris didn't do drugs, and she very rarely drank. I myself of course did both to excess. She never asked me to stop doing them or gave me an ultimatum. She just didn't partake in any of the drinking or drugs and had a good time anyway. What a concept! Having a good time without the use of drugs and alcohol! Who knew that you could actually do that? I evidently didn't back then. Not yet anyway. All the people I hung around back then, what they did for fun was to go to bars and parties and get stoned. I guess that the saying is true that you tend to become like those you associate with.

Now Kris was no angel. (Well, she was to me.) She had done her share of wild living when she was a teenager. She had run away from home several times and got a little crazy out on the road at different times. There were even times when she had done drugs. However, she never enjoyed doing that kind of thing, so it was easy for her to give them up. She told me of some wild parties she had been to and some of the stuff she'd done.

She was a mom now though, with two little ones depending on her. She had responsibilities, and she wasn't about to let those two kids down. Kris had been through some rough times and had been abandoned by her husband several times in some rather bad situations. She had been left alone with two kids in unfamiliar towns with no money and not knowing a soul around. There was no one she could call or count on. She wound up having to make some hard decisions to take care of her children. When it happened again in Ft. Meyers, Florida, she had enough. She swallowed her pride and called her father for help. Hoyt sent her a bus ticket and some money and told her she and the kids could come and stay at home until she got back on her feet.

To say Kris was a little cautious or leery of men was an understatement. She was very guarded. Now there I came, a big, bushy-haired biker who worked at a garage *and* as a bouncer at a *bar*. Yes, she was extremely skeptical. She told her sister and Carroll that she was in no hurry to jump into another relationship. She was going to wait until she felt right about it—about us. With the way I was living, who could blame her?

On our fourth date, I suggested that we take the kids with us. She was a bit surprised about that, but she agreed. I asked the kids where they would like to go, and they picked McDonalds and the park. They loved it, and surprisingly, so did I. I always considered myself just a big kid anyway. We went and had hamburgers and fries and then went and played at the park. I got to be with the kids on their level. We had a blast swinging on the swings and going down the slides. I even went on the little merry-go-round ride at the park with them. They had a great time. So did I! They were so much fun to be with!

Kris and I still hadn't been intimate yet. We had just been talking and kissing. That was very unusual for me. I was usually gone if it didn't happen right away. There was something different this time—something special. I was starting to feel different than I had ever felt with anyone else. Evidently she felt something different too. She still kept me waiting though. She said she wanted to (and so did I!), but she wanted to make sure I was going to stick around. She wanted to be appreciated for her and not just a quick thrill and then be done with.

After we were, though, I was hooked! I spent as much time as I could with Kris and the kids. I would ride over after work during the week and hang out with them. Sometimes we would go to the park or a walk. There were times when we took the kids for ice cream or we would just hang out and watch TV. I lived about fifteen miles from her, so our time together was sometimes limited. I enjoyed every minute of it I could. She loved it too, and I know Nick and Kerstin did. They got to be a part of most of the things we did together.

We couldn't go far when we had the kids with us. I only had my bike. Kris had a car, but it needed a lot of work. It was an older car and was falling apart. That was right up my alley. I would get her car fixed up so we could all go together and do stuff. It kept breaking down and needed major work. Up until then, I would borrow someone else's car, and once in a while Hoyt let us use his. Kris and her sisters were amazed. That had *never* happened before.

A funny thing happened while all this was going on. The lifestyle I was leading had begun to change. The crowd I was running with I saw less and less. My drug and alcohol consumption went *way* down. I was smoking pot once in a while and just drinking on the weekends and mainly when I was working at the bar. Kris would come to the bar sometimes to just hang out. I had been working at the bar for over a year, and there weren't very many fights anymore. I made sure of that. My main duties involved checking IDs at the door for under aged people trying to get in, like I was when I started there. After midnight there wasn't a lot for me to do, so we would play pinball or I would try to teach her how to shoot pool.

Some of the girls at the bar and some of the waitresses didn't like Kris hanging out there. They were no longer getting my attention like they used to. I would be friendly and sometimes would even flirt with them (although it didn't seem to happen much with Kris looking), but that was as far as it went. I was totally into Kris, and she was totally into me.

One night after work there, was going to be a party at the DJ's house. Kris was working late that night and didn't get off until 2:30. She had a part-time job at McDonalds and had to close. I called her and asked her to come with me. She said she was tired and needed a shower so maybe another time. Several of the girls who hung out at the bar and a few of the waitresses were going, and I was elected as one of the drivers because I was driving a friend's car. The DJ lived just about a half a mile from where Kris worked.

On the way there, one of the waitresses named Linda found out Kris wasn't going and concocted a plan to make her jealous and said, "Oh, let's just stop by and see if she wants to go anyway."

She was riding in the backseat. I thought it couldn't hurt to ask her one more time, so I swung by there. When I pulled up, Linda jumped in the front seat and started hanging all over me, and Kris saw it. She said she still didn't want to go and told me to go and have a good time. She was very friendly and pleasant. I was pushing Linda off of me and told Kris that I was *not* going to the party with Linda. I was elected as driver, and she wound up in my car. She said we would talk later. She was calm and didn't let it show, but I knew she was pissed.

I drove to the party and let Linda know that her ploy didn't work, and I was *not* going to be with her. There was no way I was going to cheat on Kris, and what she did *sucked*!

She said, "Oh, did I do something wrong? I thought you were going to the party with me."

I said "Yeah, BS. You just wanted to get a rise out of Kris. It didn't work, though, did it?"

The next day I tried to call her. Kris wouldn't accept my calls. Yeah, she was pissed. That evening I rode over there and tried to explain what had happened. She didn't want to talk. I tried to talk to her, to explain what was going on. I tried to tell her that this was Linda's plan to make Kris jealous and split us up, all to no avail. She wasn't having it. She saw Linda hanging on me and was fit to be tied. I left to go home. I knew she would calm down sooner or later (at least I hoped so).

One of the waitresses at the bar and Kris had become friends. Her name was Beverly, but everyone called her Boom Boom. I'll just allow you to use your imagination as to why we called her that. Kris called her after I left to talk to her, and Bev told her the whole thing. She told her that since Kris and I had started dating that I wasn't paying Linda any attention and she couldn't stand it. I never went out with Linda anyway. I may have flirted a few times, but that was it.

Boom Boom came up with a rather brilliant idea to get back at Linda. Kris was looking for another job. The bar was looking for another waitress. Kris could make good money and "Be there to keep an eye on him" as she put it. Boom Boom was great. She knew I was faithful to Kris, and she told her that. But she also told her, "You can't be too careful, and sometimes it's best to keep them on a short leash."

Kris started working there the next week. Linda got pissed when the owner, Joe, gave Kris her section. Kris just said, "Aww, poor baby." Linda wound up quitting the next week.

The longer Kris and I were together, the more I fell for her. And I didn't just fall for Kris; I fell for the whole package: Kris, Nick, and

Kerstin. I loved it all! By Christmas that year, I told Kris that I was in love with her. She was hesitant, and she said "Yeah, but what about the kids?"

I said "Are you kidding? I love them too!"

Kris sighed and said "Wow, I never thought this would happen. I never dreamed anyone would want me with my two kids. I love you too! I have for a while. I just didn't want to say anything because I thought that I would scare you off if I told you how I felt."

She loved me too! Wow, what a great night that was!

Love, ain't it grand!

Chapter 4

Becoming a Changed Man

LOVE HAS A WAY OF CHANGING A PERSON. Most of the time it's for the better. I know it was for me. Before I met Kris, my life was getting out of control. All the drinking, drugs, fights, illegal activity, and bike stunts I pulled were just getting more dangerous. I didn't think so at the time, but looking back now, I can't imagine how I survived. God had a plan for me, and I know that it was only by His grace that I made it through those days.

Hanging out with those bikers made me feel cool, like I belonged to something larger than myself. I wanted to prove myself to them and fit in. I wanted their respect, so I would do things to excess to try to fit in and get noticed. I thought the best way to do that was to push things farther than they did. If they drank a beer, I drank two. If they took a shot of tequila, I would chug from the bottle. If they did drugs, I did more. If one of the guys did a stunt on a bike like riding a wheelie or taking a jump, I would try to do the wheelie longer and make the jump farther. They would laugh and thought it was great, I thought I was being "cool." I learned later that I was like their big pet.

When I started doing stuff for the gang like going on runs, carrying drugs from one place to another, and taking care of the station and car lot they owned, I thought I was living large. I was making a lot of money and had access to plenty of drugs. I was going to all the parties and bars. Sex, drugs, and rock and roll were the things that kept me going. All I was really doing was getting a bad reputation. By the time I was nineteen, just before I met Kris, I had a list of traffic offenses a page and a half long. I was being watched by the police because they knew who I was running with and what they did. They would pull me over all the time, hoping to catch me with something on me. They never did though. They would get pissed because I would just laugh at them. There were a couple times when I even ran from them just to see if I could get away on my bike. I did. However, they knew where I lived, and they just waited for me to go home and came in and arrested me there. As I said before, a lot of people thought the way I was living that I would either be dead or in prison by the time I turned twenty-one. If I had kept living that way, they would have probably been right.

After Kris and I started dating that all started to change. The drinking and the drug use went way down. Little by little I started to calm down and not take as many risks. I was fighting less even at the bar. Working as a bouncer, I learned to talk my way out of most of the situations where I would normally just bust a guy's head open. I stopped hanging around my biker buddies as much and told them I didn't have time to go on the runs or do a lot of the other stuff with them. I never officially became a member of the club. Technically I was just what they would call a "hang around," so that never became an issue. I wasn't working at that station or the car lot anymore and had a job in a different garage. Even at the bar I was drinking way less and not going to the parties or the after-hours clubs.

I had a new focus in life. I felt I had something and someone to live for. Kris never asked me to stop all that stuff or to change my lifestyle. It just happened. She accepted me as I was with all my imperfections.

The more time I spent with Kris, the less I was interested in doing the things I'd done before. She got to where she loved riding on my motorcycle too. The first time she rode with me, which was her first time on a bike, she was a bit scared. After a couple of rides she fell in love with it, and we rode together all the time. The only problem was that we couldn't take the kids with us on the motorcycle. I took them each on rides, and they loved it too. However, if we wanted to go out somewhere with the kids, we had to find alternate transportation so all of us could go. Kris had her old car, but it was on its last legs and was always breaking down. The only transportation I had was the bike, so I started trading vehicles with a buddy of mine. He loved to ride but rarely got the chance, so I would use his car and he would use my bike on some weekends. That was another major change for me. *Nobody* ever touched my bike! Kris loved his car though. It was a dark-blue '69 Pontiac Grand Prix, and it was nice. She enjoyed riding in that car and appreciated the fact that I would go to all the trouble to trade vehicles just so we could take Nick and Kerstin with us. She knew how much I loved to ride and how big of a deal it was for me to let someone else ride my bike. This went on for several months, with my friend and I trading on most weekends.

Then my friend came up with a radical transaction for me to consider. He made an offer to me one day when we were going to trade vehicles for the weekend and said, "I love your bike, and you like my car. Would you consider a trade? Even up, my car for your bike." I loved riding, but I found that I loved Kris and the kids more. I didn't even hesitate and said "Sure!" I thought that would be the solution so I could be with Kris and the kids more often and have reliable transportation for us.

Love can make you do things you never thought you would do. Not only that, but you actually enjoy doing those things because of how you feel and the way you see things when you are in love. That's the way it was with us anyway. Love—true love—makes you want to be a better person. It makes you see things from a whole new perspective. With Kris and the kids, it was like I found myself. There was a purpose for my life. I was starting to become the man I was meant to be. I could feel that down in my very soul! Weekends went from being a big, drunken party to picnics at the park and going to the beach with Kris and the kids. We would go to the drive-in movies (remember them?) and take Nick and Kerstin for ice cream. Sometimes we took them fishing, and we would go back to the house, where I would clean and cook our catch. I loved every minute of it! I had found true love, or it had found me!

The great thing was, she found it too! We found each other. Neither one of us was looking for it. Neither of us expected it, but here it was. *True love*—that special thing that so many people strive for and look for and listen to in all those "silly love songs." We had found the type of love that movies are made about and songs and poems are written about. We had found *true love* with each other. That special kind of love took a single mom of two, struggling to make it on her own and down on relationships, into a beautiful, vibrant young lady who was smiling again and happy for the first time in a long time. It took a big, bad, drug-crazed and drunken biker (on the outside) into a big teddy bear, a big kid, and a gentleman (on the inside, I was still kinda rough around the edges). Who would have believed it? I know that if you would have told me before I met Kris that this would happen, I would have told you that you were crazy. It happened, though, and completely changed my life!

> *Love—true love—can change people.*
> *It changed me!*

Chapter 5

The Kids

WHEN I FIRST HEARD THE IDEA OF GOING out with Kris, a big red flag for me was the fact that she had two kids already. I was young and wild, so the last thing I thought that would give me pleasure was being around two little kids. It did though. It was truly amazing to me how much fun I had with Nick and Kerstin. I really enjoyed having them around and getting to spend time with them and play with them. To see the pure joy in their faces as they ran around having a great time and just being kids was an awesome experience for me. It did help that I am just a big kid at heart and always have been.

Initially it was a bit scary to me to have the kids with us. I had never done this kind of thing before—being responsible and taking care of kids that is. Now here I was with two little ones to watch over and keep safe. That just wasn't me, or at least I didn't think so back then. However, after the first few times taking them to the park, all that apprehension disappeared. They ran around and played, going on the swings, the slide, and the merry-go-round. I ran right along with them. I thought, *Wow, these kids are a blast! Who knew?* We had a great time together.

Kris was amazed too. She had never expected this. She was afraid the kids would be a deal breaker for her. She thought that anyone she dated would find out about the kids and turn and run away. She told me that she thought they would be the reason I would let her down and leave her like her ex-husband had done. Yet here I was, running around playing with her kids and having a ball.

At first she thought I might be putting on a front. She thought that I was just using the kids to impress her and get us closer and trying to get into her pants (which did cross my mind, by the way). However, when I started planning our dates and including the kids even when she had arranged a babysitter, she knew it was real and that I genuinely enjoyed spending time with her *and* the kids. I loved these two little guys. (Oops, one girl. Sorry, Kerstin.) They really enjoyed being with us too. After all, those kids had been through a lot. They'd been abandoned by their father and left alone in strange places right along with Kris. Nick and Kerstin never really had much of an opportunity up to that point to just be kids. So when they got the chance to be with us and get out and just be kids, they loved it!

After about five or six times of taking them with us, Nick came home and asked his mom in front of me, "Can we call Bill daddy?" Talk about melting my heart!

Kris said "No, this is Bill."

He turned and said, "Darn!" and walked away.

After we had been dating for about six months, I knew that I loved Kris. There was absolutely no doubt in my mind that I had fallen head over heels in love with this amazing woman. It was that forever kind of love, and I knew it! I loved Nick and Kerstin too. I fell in love with the whole package. I knew I wanted to spend the rest of my life with them and I wanted to be their dad. I wanted to marry Kris and start a new life together. About a month later, I asked Kris's father for his daughter's hand in marriage.

He said, "Well, I think that's a question for her, isn't it?"

I said, "Yes, sir, but you are her father, and I thought it only right to ask for your blessing first, before I asked her."

Hoyt said, "So you haven't asked her yet?"

I said, "No, sir. I respect your opinion and didn't want to ask her before I talked to you."I knew that he was an old-school type of man, and he appreciated the fact that I asked him first. He smiled and gave me his blessing.

The following weekend we would have the house to ourselves. Kris's parents and younger sister were going on a trip to Alabama to see their family for a week. I thought that would be the perfect time to ask her. I planned the whole weekend for us.I had purchased the ring and told Kris that I was going to cook dinner for all of us that weekend. My dad was a professional chef, and I learned how to cook at an early age. I can still remember the menu that I planned. It consisted of fried lemon pepper chicken made with fresh chicken breast, lemon pepper gravy, mashed potatoes, mixed vegetables, and strawberry shortcake for desert. It wasn't exactly a culinary masterpiece, but it got the job done. Kris was impressed at the fact that I could cook and would go to all the trouble of preparing that dinner for us.

We all ate together in the dining room that evening, and they loved it. They enjoyed the chicken, and we finished the meal off with the strawberry shortcake. After dinner, we all went into the living room and watched TV for a while. Then we put the kids to bed. Kris and I went back and sat on the couch to watch TV some more until we knew they were asleep. After about an hour, I got up and went into the kitchen and told her that I was going to put the leftovers away and clean up a bit. Before dinner I took the time to hide the ring in the pantry so I could retrieve it after the kids were asleep and complete the evening with my proposal. I called out for Kris and asked her to come in to the kitchen and give me a hand with something.

When she had just come through the door of the kitchen, I got down on one knee, took her by the hand and said, "Krista Joy (her middle name), will you marry me?"

She put her hand over her mouth and gasped. She was shocked! This was nothing that was expected. She looked me in the eyes, broke out into a huge smile, and said, "Yes, I'll marry you!" I put the ring on her finger, and we kissed. She said "Wow, and you can cook too! What a bargain!"

Just then we heard a noise behind us. We looked and saw Nick scurrying back off to the bedroom. Evidently he had gotten up out of bed and was standing behind Kris the whole time. He stopped right at the doorway going back to the bedroom, gave us a thumb's up, and said, "*Yes!*" Then he went back to bed. The next morning at breakfast Nick said, "Can we call Bill daddy now?"

Kris smiled with her big, sexy smile and said, "Yes, you can call him daddy now!"

They both yelled, "*Yeah!*" and ran over and hugged us both.

It's really unbelievable how good love can make you feel. When you find love, true love, the entire world looks brighter. The songs you hear have more meaning as you listen to the words. You start to see this great big, beautiful world as an awesome place where dreams really do come true. The highs that love can take you to far outweigh the lows, or at least that's been my experience. To see Kris's face when I proposed was truly incredible and an experience I will never forget. It is permanently etched in my mind. Then to see the excitement in Nick and Kerstin's faces the next morning was wonderful! Knowing that they wanted me to be their daddy was inspiring. It brought joy to my heart! No wonder Jesus loved little kids so much.

Love makes this life worth living!

Chapter 6

I Do–We Did

KRIS AND I DATED FOR A WHILE LONGER after we became engaged. My transformation to become a better man continued too. Shortly after that, we both stopped working at the bar. Kris got a job at Publix Supermarket, and I was working at a different auto-repair garage. I had already traded my bike for the Grand Prix, so we were able to spend time together as a family. Wow, that was something I never thought would happen! I loved riding my bike, but I loved Kris and the kids more. The car she had was very unreliable and one thing after another would break, and when it did, that would leave her without a way to work. Even though I was a mechanic, I wasn't a miracle worker. Her car was very old and had a *lot* of miles on it. It was an old Pontiac Bonneville and had definitely seen better days. That summer I bought Kris a used car for her birthday. I got a good deal on it and went through the car completely, making sure that she could depend on it to get her to work and the kids around. It was a '69 Mercury, and she loved it. Her car had finally died, and she had to have reliable transportation.

Our friends and family were against us getting married at first, especially mine. They knew me, the old me, and knew that this thing

I was feeling just couldn't be real. They were also worried because Kris had the kids. They wondered why I would want to take on someone else's responsibility and tie myself down with a ready-made family. They also worried about the kids because they knew the life I had been leading up to that time, and that life was not conducive to kids. After they saw us together for a while and the way we were together and that we really loved each other and that I also loved the kids, their fears and worries dissipated. They started to become genuinely happy and supportive of us. They saw the changes I had made and were relieved and thought that maybe I was finally calming down and becoming a responsible adult. Love had tamed the wild beast in me.

It wasn't very long after this that Kris and I decided to move in together. We were spending all our spare time together anyway. By getting a place of our own, we would get to spend more time together and save time and money at the same time(that was my reasoning and how I sold her on the idea).We got an apartment in Pinellas Park and moved our family into it. Kris and I hadn't set a date to get married yet, and actually I wasn't even thinking of a date. I mean,I had the girl, we had the kids, we were engaged, we were living together, and we were happy. I thought that was enough, at least for now. Nick and Kerstin were calling me daddy, and I loved it. I loved being a dad, and I still do. After all, I was just a big kid. (Sometimes I still am!) I figured that we were playing the part of a married couple and a family. We were young, in love, and happy. Why did we need a piece of paper to make it legal?

Just after the first of the year in 1978, I was working for Firestone as a mechanic and a service driver for their road service truck. Kris and I had been living together for about six months. One night while we were in bed, she started bleeding and having a discharge. It wasn't that time of the month or that type of bleeding. This was worse. After a short while, the bleeding and discharge stopped, and she said she was fine. She said she felt fine and everything was okay. I wanted her to get to the doctor to get checked out anyway. She didn't want to but I insisted, and the next morning I called her sister Kay and asked if she would take her. She said she would. I wanted to make sure someone took her because I had to work, and I didn't want Kris to drive herself. I also wanted to make sure she went. Kay came over that morning, and she took Kris to see the doctor.

Later that day I got a call from Kris. She asked if I could take a little time off and come over to Kay's house to talk. I asked what was wrong and the doctor had to say. All she would tell me was that she needed to speak to me and she didn't want to do it over the phone. She said she was fine and just needed to talk to me. Naturally I thought the worst and that there was something seriously wrong with her. I immediately took a break from work and drove over to Kay's house. When I got there, Kay and her friend Deanna were there and seemed to have concerned looks on their faces.

I said, "Okay, what's going on? What's wrong?"

Kris looked at me and said, "Sit down. I have something to tell you."

My heart sank! All I could think of at the time was, *What is she going to tell me? What was all that bleeding actually from, and what was the cause? Does she have a disease, or is she dying? What is going on here?* I was expecting her to tell me some devastating news. I was expecting her to tell me that she didn't have long to live.

I sat down, and she came over, took me by the hand, looked at me, and said, "Bill, I'm pregnant."

I sat there for a second and let that sink in. This was definitely not the news I was expecting to hear. All this time I was thinking of the worst-case scenario. Did Kris just say what I thought she said? Just then a huge smile broke out on my face, and I said "That's great! I'm gonna be a daddy again!" I got up and hugged and kissed her and said, "Well, I guess this means we're going to have to set a wedding date."

Kris started to cry. She said, "I thought you'd be upset. I thought you might even leave me if I had another child. I have been worried about it since I found out and afraid to tell you."

"Oh, baby. How could I do that?" I said. "I love you! I love the kids! You've made me the happiest man in the world!"

She wanted to tell me this at Kay's house because she actually thought I would leave her if I knew she was pregnant and having another kid. She felt she needed back up and support. I guess she expected that because of the experience she had with her previous marriage and other relationships. She was very happily surprised.

My love for Kris grew that day and hers for me. It's amazing how that can and does happen. You believe you love someone. The love you feel for them is so real and so enormous. You think there is no possible way you could love them more than you already do. Then something happens, and your love grows even more, even stronger, even bigger than before. Your heart grows, and you *are* able to love them more! The intimacy and closeness you feel is incredible. God really knew what He was doing when He created us so long ago to be partners, man and wife, and helpers for each other. I didn't know God at the time, but I can sure see His plan for us now! He brought Kris and me together and had us fall in love and start our lives together. Hindsight is twenty/twenty, right?

We set our wedding date as June 10, 1978. The ceremony took place in my parents' yard. The wedding took place on the side of the house, and we held the reception on the other side. On that sunny June day in front of our family and friends, we said our vows and became husband and wife. We were only able to take a very short honeymoon as I had just started a new job and Kris was six months along at the time of the wedding. My brother Bob was my best man, and Kris's sister Kay was her maid of honor. She was a beautiful bride, and I was a happy groom!

We had been saving our money to go toward the wedding, and we wanted to have our own place to raise our growing family. Shortly after we were married, we purchased our first home together in July. At the end of August, our son Jeremy was born. Our family was growing, and I felt that our journey as a family had just begun.

Years ago Frank Sinatra had a song that said, "Love and marriage, love and marriage, they go together like a horse and carriage. This I tell you brother, you can't have one without the other!"

Love and marriage—what a great combination!

Chapter 7

The Young Family and Miracles

WE WERE JUST STARTING OUT AS A FAMILY, and things were going well. We had just purchased our first home. It was a little three-bedroom, one-bath house on a corner lot. The house was an ugly green color with white shutters, a good-sized yard, a carport, and a screened-in front porch. We knew we could make it look like our own home with just a little paint and carpet. The possibilities seemed endless as we discussed the things we would do and the improvements we would make. The house was locatedin south St. Petersburg near the town of Gulfport. The neighborhood was nice and had a very diverse cross-section of people living there. Between myself, Kris, Nick, Kerstin, and Jeremy, the house was very full. That little house was full of love.

I was working as a mechanic at a local garage, and Kris stayed home with the kids. We had discussed this and looked into the possibility of her working outside the home,but financially it made more sense for her to be a stay-at-home mom. The kids would benefit by having her home, and if she took a job, she would only be bringing home about $40 a week after taxes and babysitting costs. She was very happy with the decision, and she loved being a mom. Kris was an excellent mother. She did take in a few kids to babysit during the week for extra money. That only lasted a couple of months, though. The other mothers started to take advantage of Kris by not paying her on time and not picking their kids up when they were supposed to. When they did this, it would frustrate Kris, and it would cut in on our family time. Our family time was very important to us, as was our alone time after the kids went to bed. We made the decision to fire those parents after one mother left her child with us until 11:00p.m. when she was supposed to be there by 5:30. Being able to stay home with the kids was an option Kris never had before.She really enjoyed it. Things were tight, but we made it work. The love we shared and the happiness we had more than made up for it.

In the spring we attended a family reunion with Hoyt's family, who came down from Georgia. They were a very musical family, and at the reunion they, broke out the guitars and played the piano. They were singing gospel songs and singing old hymns. They were also a religious family, and one of Kris's aunts read some verses out of the Bible and said some things about Jesus and how He came and died on the cross for our sins. Kris accepted Christ as her Savior that day. Her cousin Dwight invited us to go to church with them the following Sunday, so we did. We really enjoyed it, and the following week, the pastor made a visit to our home. He had heard about our family reunion and what had taken place and about Kris accepting Christ. He then talked to me about it. I had never heard much about God or Jesus growing up. We may have attended church two or three times in my whole life. When he read me those Bible verses, though, something came over me. I knew I was a sinner (with my past, that was a given), and I needed forgiveness. That night in our home I prayed and asked Jesus into my heart. We began attending every Sunday, and over time we became very involved in the church. We enjoyed the people and quickly made friends with several other families and with the pastor and his family. Kris began to sing in the choir and help in the nursery. She always loved babies. I became an usher and sometimes on Saturday a bus mechanic. After a while we were spending Sunday morning, Sunday night, Wednesday night, and part of Saturday there. I know that for us a close and personal relationship with God was helping us survive financially and drew us closer together.

During those days, we were witnesses to miracles happening around us. Prayers were being answered for people in the church, and people were healed from cancer. This was not a holy roller church, and they didn't have healing services. This was a Baptist church that really be- lieved in the power of prayer. They would have special days of prayer and sometimes even a day of fasting and prayer. We had our own miracle happen in our family with our son Jeremy. When he was just about eighteen months old, we had an accident that there is no way on this earth he should have survived. Even the doctors, nurses, and the staff at the hospital were at a loss to try and explain how he survived.

One evening I came home from work, and Kris was fixing dinner. She asked if I would run to the store and pick up some milk and bread. I said "Sure, no problem." I walked out to get in the van, and Jeremy followed right behind me. I told him to go back in the house. He turned and started back in the house, so I went to the van. I looked and he was following me again, so I told him, "No, you can't come with me. Go back in the house." He turned a headed for the front door. This happened again, so I picked him up and carried him back to the house and put him inside and told him he had to stay here and not to come after me again. He said, "Okay, Daddy, see ya later," and went running toward his room. I again left to go to the store. I went out and got in the van. It was an ugly purple van, one of those old Ford vans with the front that is flat. When you are in the driver's seat, you are basically sitting almost right against the windshield. It was my work van, and it was parked on the grass on the side of our house. I started it up and began to pull away. Just then I felt the front right tire run over something. I knew there was nothing there when I parked in that spot earlier, so I went a little further, and I felt the right rear tire run over something. I looked out at the side mirror and saw Jeremy lying on the ground. I had just run over my son!

I freaked out and just jumped out of the van and ran to Jeremy and scooped him up in my arms. I started yelling for Kris, hollering for her to call 911. I screamed out that I had just killed our son and began to cry and wail! Normally I am the calm one when there is a crisis. I couldn't do that this time. Kris took that role and did it magnificently. She ran to see what happened and then immediately called 911. Then she called her mother and sister to come and watch the kids while we went to the hospital. She then called the pastor of our church and told him what happened and asked him to pray. He said he would and would get their members and other churches to pray also.

When the ambulance arrived, Kris told the paramedics what had happened. They took Jeremy and put him on a stretcher and started checking him out immediately. They took his vital signs and radioed in to the hospital and gave them the information and told them an ETA for the ambulance to get there. Kris then rode with Jeremy to the hospital, and I waited for her mom to come and take care of Nick and Kerstin. She got there in just a few minutes, but it seemed like an eternity. I was still so frantic, so afraid that I had killed my son that I couldn't even think straight. Kris's mom, Nadine, tried to calm me down a bit. She told me she would take care of the kids and I should just go! With Nick and Kerstin taken care of, I jumped in our car and rushed off like a screaming banshee to get to the hospital with Kris and Jeremy. I made it there just a few minutes after they arrived.

In the emergency room the attending nurse asked what happened, and I told her that I had run Jeremy over with my van. I told her I felt both the front and rear wheels run over him. The abrasions were on his head, so she said there was no way that the van ran over his head. "If that had happened, he would be dead," she said. She said the van must have knocked him down and brushed his head with the bumper or something.

She didn't believe that the van could have actually run him over. God took care of that and made sure she believed. Within a few minutes, a big bruise in the perfect shape of a tire track appeared on the side of Jeremy's face. It covered the entire right side of his head. They were all astonished by this and started rushing around running tests and taking x-rays.

About this time Jeremy started slipping into a coma, and they didn't think he would live much longer. The attending physician told us that he had called the neurosurgeon who was on call, but he said he was attending an event in another city and he couldn't be there before 9:00 p.m. It was now just 6:30p.m. They said they would do everything they could, but they were expecting the worst. By this time Jeremy was no longer conscious. We were devastated by this and couldn't believe what was happening. Kris and I held each other and wept.

A short time later we were told that one of the top neurosurgeons in the state had stopped by the hospital to see a patient and had heard about Jeremy. He came down to see if he could help. Even in our darkest hours, God can show His love for us. This doctor looked at the scenario and asked what had been done so far. He ordered a CAT scan and a MRI and brought Kris and me into a consultation room to inform us as to what was going on with our son.

He said, "Under the circumstances, it's a miracle he is still alive. The vehicle definitely ran over his head. The bruise is proof enough of that. We are not sure he is going to make it through the night. If he does survive, I need you to be prepared. There will be some brain damage, some internal hemorrhaging, and a severe bruise of the brain. I've ordered some tests and should have the results back in a couple of hours. I will call you back here then and go over the results." We were crying as we thanked him.

Kris and I were devastated. We thought we were losing our son. We hugged each other and cried. We didn't know what to do! We walked outside and held each other, and I began to pray. I prayed that God would reach down and heal our son. Then I stopped, looked up to heaven, and said, "God, thank You for giving us Jeremy. We dedicated him to You a while back now. You gave him to us, and we are grateful for the time we have had with him. You gave him to us, and now we are giving him back to You. Take care of him. We put him in Your care. We willingly give him back to You. Help to give us a peace about it. But God, we would sure like to keep him a while longer."

Right after we prayed that prayer, we felt a peace come over us. We looked at each other, and we both felt it. I had never felt anything like it before. We knew he was in God's hands, and we were willing to accept God's will. If that meant Jeremy would no longer be with us, we were going to be okay with that.

Our pastor had arrived a short time later, and we told him the situation. He told us the whole church was praying, as were several other churches in the area.

An hour later the doctor called us back into the consultation room. He had the results back much sooner than he had expected. Then he said, "I can't explain it, I don't understand it and frankly, I can't believe it, but there is no brain damage. There is no internal hemorrhaging, and there is no bruise of the brain. The only things we can see that happened are some scratches and that bruise on the side of his face. There is some very slight swelling around his brain that is common after someone gets hit on the head or other head injury, but it is minor. God must really be watching over him." He told us we could go in and see our son.

When we got in there, Jeremy had come out of the coma and was awake and alert. He was lying there on the bed, and he was answering questions by shaking his head yes and no. They told us he would have to stay there in the intensive care unit for about a week. After two days, they couldn't keep him down any longer and allowed him to walk around the intensive care unit pushing around his IV pole. One week to the day of the accident Jeremy walked out of that hospital without a mark on him. There were other people there who had less severe bruising thanJeremy and theirs were still there. The Lord healed him completely. He is our miracle child and an example of God's love.

Love is grand, and God's love is forever. It can work miracles!

Chapter 8

Trial by Fire

WITH JEREMY HEALED AND HOME, THINGS got back to normal. With a growing family and trying to maintain our home, the financial demands grew. I started doing some work in the evenings on friends' and church members' cars for extra money. I also started to buy and sell cars and motorcycles. The extra income was just what we needed at the time. Another answered prayer.

After about a year or so Kris started talking about having another baby. She worked in the nursery at church taking care of other babies and desired to have another one of our own. She even started picking out names. We discussed it, and I didn't think it was the right time (it never is) to enlarge our family. Kris agreed but was secretly praying for a baby girl. She prayed for one with long brown hair and big brown eyes. God was listening and answered her prayers.

Kris was on birth control, but as they say, "Nothing with birth control is 100 percent effective except abstinence," and *that* was out of the question! She became pregnant with our fourth child. On February 5, 1982, Anita Renee Kyne was born. We had two names picked out, and when we first saw her when she was delivered, Kris and I looked at each other and at the same time said, "Anita!" Our family grew again. Our love grew again—our love for each other, our love for our family, and our love for God.

It's amazing how that can happen. You love someone or something so much and you don't think you can love anymore, and then, as if by magic, your love grows. It gets taken to another level. You find that you have even more capacity in your heart to love your wife, your children, your family, and your God. At least that is the way it has been for me. That is the way it's been for the love we shared as a family.

Our lives seemed to be going very well. We were still very active in church. I had taken a job in Clearwater as a manager of a service station, and I had started buying and selling cars on the side. The extra income was just what we needed for our growing family. Our church had started a school, and our kids were enrolled there. Kris was recruited to be the teacher for the pre-K kids, and doing that paid for their tuition. The one thing we were missing was health insurance. I had asked my employer about it, but being a small business owner, he couldn't afford to offer that.

A short time later I had an opportunity to go to work for the city of St. Petersburg as a mechanic. The pay was less, but the benefit package was what I thought we needed for our growing family. Plus the fact that the job was much closer to home and Kris wouldn't have to do as much driving. As it was we only had one car, so Kris was driving three hours a day to get me to and from work and the kids to school. This job cut the commute in half.

Things began to change in our lives. The cut in pay was taking its toll, and I wasn't able to buy and sell cars as I was before. The financial pressure was making things a bit tense at home. Kris wanted to help by going to work, but once again it wasn't feasible with having four kids and having to pay for daycare. Things at church were changing too. There was a change in leadership, and the pastor stepped down and put another pastor in place. Because I was in a place of leadership myself at the time, being a deacon and Sunday school teacher, I could see that things were not being done like they should. Some of the finances of the church were being diverted to places they shouldn't go, and people were doing things that just weren't right in the church. I tried to talk to the pastor about it but was basically told to mind my own business.

I wasn't the only one who saw what was going on. Others in the church did too and came to me with their concerns. They had also asked the pastor and were told the same thing. There was a group of people who wanted the new pastor to step down. They came to me and wanted me to take over the job of pastor. I told them that I was in no way qualified for that. I did feel God's call on my life but didn't feel I was ready for that responsibility. The church was at a crossroads. I couldn't in good conscience stay at the church with the things that were going on. I didn't want to split the church either. Our family had a choice to make. We could stay and split the church or step aside and try and find another church. We decided to step down and move on.

Things went from bad to worse financially as I was injured at work as well. I was in the manufacturing shop, and a machine I was using broke and sent me flying across the shop into a wall. The next thing I remembered was waking up in the hospital. Thank God nothing was broken, but I wound up with a concussion, a separated shoulder, and back injuries. I was out of work for a while and put on workers' compensation, which only paid 60 percent of my pay. We were already taking home much less than I was used to making, so this decrease took a toll on our finances.

At about this same time Kris's father became ill and went into the hospital. Over the course of the next few months, we spent a lot of time in doctors' offices and the hospital between my rehab and Hoyt's hospitalization. On one trip to see him, he called me into his room alone. He wanted to talk to me privately. He knew he was dying and asked if I would look after Nadine when he was gone and take care of things around the house for her. I told him that I would. Hoyt passed away a few days later.

Kris's parents had an older home, and there was quite a lot of work to be done on it. I was over there doing repairs on it several times a week. Kris's mom, Nadine, tried to pay me for the work, but I wouldn't accept her money and told her that I promised Hoyt I would take care of things for her. Our financial problems were growing, and I was still not released to go back to work. I felt I was ready, but the doctors wouldn't let me. We were going to lose our house if we didn't do something pretty soon. Nadine came over one evening with an offer. She was alone in that big house, and we were over there several times a week. She said we should move in with her and sell our house. That way she would feel better about not paying me and we could save money at the same time. We agreed to give it a try.

With mounting physical, financial, spiritual, and emotional pressure, things were getting worse in our relationship. Kris and I began to argue over things. She wasn't happy having to live back at her parents' house again. Our bills were still piling up, and there didn't seem to be an end in sight. By this time, we had tried a few other churches, and none of them felt right. We had basically stopped going altogether. That was a big mistake. Instead of turning to God, we turned away and tried to handle things ourselves. After all, we thought things couldn't get much worse. *Wrong!*

The doctor finally released me to go back to work. I had been looking for a better job while I was rehabilitating and found one with Goodyear Tire and Auto. We were still living in Kris's mom's house, and on February 5, we had a birthday party for Anita. Kris and I had a disagreement about something. I don't even remember what it was. Isn't that always the way? Arguments that seem so big at the time you don't remember later. Kris left and went to a friend's house down the street. I stayed at the house with the kids and Nadine.

Later that evening I was on the couch watching TV. The kids had gone to bed, and so had Nadine. She got up and came into the living room and said, "Bill, have you been smoking marijuana?"

I said, "No, ma'am, I haven't done that in years."

She said, "I didn't think so, but I just smelled somethin' funny." Then she went back to bed.

I went back to watching TV and fell asleep on the couch. About 1:00 a.m. I was jarred awake by an explosion from the kitchen. I saw smoke coming from the back of the house and went back there to find the entire back of the house in flames! I hollered, "*Fire!*" and ran to the bedroom to get the kids. I grabbed Anita and Kerstin and got them out as I yelled for Nick and Jeremy to get up. I carried them out and went back in for the boys still yelling, **"Fire,** Mom, get up. *Fire!*" I carried them out and ran back in for Nadine. She was awakened by all the yelling and ran past me as I was going back in for her. The smoke was getting thicker, and I guess I had inhaled a lot of it as I was going in and out. I fell to my knees, coughing and choking on it. It was getting hotter and very difficult to see. I managed to crawl back out the front door on my hands and knees. Smoke was billowing out of the front door, and the entire rear of the house was engulfed in flames.

I was just starting to catch my breath when Nadine hollered, "Bill, Rebel is trapped on the side yard of the house!"

Rebel was their German shepherd, and the house was surrounded by a six-foot-tall chain link fence that had Rebel trapped. I ran back toward the house and jumped over the side of the porch where Rebel was. I tried to pick him up and put him over onto the porch, but there was so much smoke coming out the door that he was terrified and wouldn't go that way. I then grabbed him up in my arms and lifted him up over the fence and tossed him clear of the house. I then climbed over myself and escaped the flames and the smoke. Exhausted, I fell to the ground and tried to catch my breath. I looked around to make sure everyone was out and that everyone was safe.

The fire department arrived and started battling the flames. It took them over an hour to get it under control. By that time the house and everything inside was pretty much a total loss. Kris had heard the sounds of the fire trucks and saw them in front of her parents' house and came running. All the neighbors were out there, and she found us all safe on the street in front of the house and began to cry. We were all there, and we were all safe. Anita looked at the house and summed it all up when she said, "My birthday got all burned up." She was right.

That fire took most of our possessions. It took our furniture, our clothes, the kids' toys, and so on. The one thing it couldn't take was our love. In fact, it brought us closer together. In times like those you realize what is really important. We were all safe, all still alive and well. All the "things" can be replaced. The petty things we were having a disagreement about were gone. There we were on the street in front of that house as a family, as a husband and wife, and we were *very* grateful for everything we had. We had each other and our love for one another, and that was plenty!

Our love grew again!

Chapter 9

And Then There Were Five

AFTER WE SALVAGED WHAT WE COULD FROM the fire, we began the process of rebuilding our lives. The Red Cross helped us initially, and the help and support of family and friends was incredible. My new employer had helped us also, and I had just started work there. We found a place to rent that was right across the street from Nadine's house. We stayed there for about a month while we brought things out from the ashes and cleaned up what we could. It's amazing to see just how fast everything you have built over a lifetime can vanish. You also start to realize what is really important in this life. You find out who your true friends are and how important relationships can be. Not long after that, we found a place that was just what we needed a couple miles away. It was a four-bedroom, two-bath house with a mother-in-law apartment on the back. We lived in the front, and Nadine had her own space in the back and the whole thing was connected, so we were just one big happy family and also could have our privacy when we needed it. And Kris and I needed it! We had a lot of making up to do, if you know what I mean! We were always very good at that! As that Garth Brooks song "Two of a Kind" says, "Sometimes we would fight just so we could make up."

Kris and I were always a very loving couple. Right from the start of our relationship it had been that way. The love we shared with one another was very physical. I believe that was one of the reasons our love was so strong and remained so strong over the course of our lives. Even during the down times, we wanted and desired one another. We could never stay mad at each other for very long. We were too passionate for that. Either Kris would say,"Bill, are you still mad? Can we kiss and make up?" Or I would say,"Kris, can I come kiss it and make it better?" That would always lighten the mood, and we would laugh, kiss, and "Make up." Evidently during one of our "make up" sessions, our daughter Rebecca was conceived.

We were just starting to rebuild our life when we found out we were expecting again. Even though it was unexpected, we were looking forward to our new addition. We started to pick out names for our new baby girl once we knew that we were going to have another daughter. Our family was growing again, and our love was growing again. Kris was always so radiant when she was pregnant. She developed a glow about her, and her smile was incredible. This time was no different. If anything, she was more beautiful than ever to me. She was always a great mom, and she loved being a mom. I loved being a dad too. I have always said that being a dad was and is my favorite job of all time!

Things in our life from that time got much better. I attribute that to God, love, and prayer. Love and prayer can and do work miracles. We have seen that firsthand in our lives. That along with a positive attitude can go a long way in making your life better. My new job was going great too. I started buying and selling cars again. Our financial situation began to get better. We got back to God and became active in church again. That in and of itself was one of the most important things we did as a family. Then on August 6, 1986, Rebecca Joy Kyne came into the world. She was a beautiful baby girl, and we felt that our family was complete. We now had two boys and three girls. We were now a family of seven. All of our children were happy and healthy.

Because we felt that our family was complete and we wanted no more children, Kris and I discussed what we should do about permanent birth control. She could have a procedure after she delivered Rebecca, or I could go and get a vasectomy. I volunteered to get the vasectomy. I thought that was only fair. After all, Kris had gone through five pregnancies. She went through the process of her body changing five times and carrying all of them in her belly all that time. She had gone through childbirth five times now and all of them natural at that. I figured that if she could do that, the least I could do was take one for the team!

We researched quite a bit and looked for a doctor to do the procedure so I could have it done as soon as Kris and the baby were home. We had a couple of choices. One doctor was named Richard Cutter. I decided against having it done with him. Think of the name for a minute, and I think you'll see and understand why. We selected another doctor who was highly recommended.

On the day of the procedure, I went in to have it done and the doctor said, "So you're here to get fixed, huh?"

I said, "No, doc, I'm here to get it broke. It works too good. You had better make sure it still shoots blanks though!"

We laughed, and he said "Yeah, I guess with five kids it does work pretty good. Don't worry, you'll be able to use it again in six weeks." He then started the procedure, and he got the job done.

Well, needless to say, we didn't wait the six weeks. I'm not sure exactly how long we did wait, but just a few weeks later, we tested it and it worked just fine. Kris and I loved each other so much, and as I said, we were always very passionate and physical. Now the added benefit of not having to worry about birth control brought out a whole new element to our love. There seemed to be an additional dimension to our passion toward each other and even more intimacy in our lovemaking. Even though we were always quite amorous together, this seemed to bring out a new level of joy, passion, and trust to our relationship. It served as a springboard to a new era and a fresh new wave of intimate pleasures for us.

Love is the gift that keeps on giving!

Chapter 10

Ten Years and Counting!

TIME MARCHES ON FOR EVERYONE, AND IT did for us as well. Our life as a family was going very well. My job was going good, and our income from side work and selling cars was keeping us where we made a very comfortable living. We were once again volunteering at church, and Kris was the kindergarten teacher at the school as well as singing in the choir. I was a Sunday school teacher and in charge of the teens at church. Our kids were involved with different activities at church, and we were one big, happy family.

One of the things that kept Kris and I so in love was good communication and paying attention to each other's wants, needs, and desires. She knew the things that I liked and I knew the things that she liked, right down to the style and color of the clothes we wore. We went shopping together when we needed clothes and would help each other pick stuff out. I enjoyed helping her pick out her clothes. After all, when it comes down to it, I was the one who benefited from the style of clothes she wore and the way things fit her. I'm the one who got to see my beautiful wife in them more than anyone else. Why wouldn't I want to help in the process?

We were coming up on our ten-year anniversary. Ten years as a couple is a very special anniversary. I knew I had to come up with something to make sure this anniversary would be something to remember. It had to be something unique and a memory that would let her know how much I loved her. I had some vacation time coming, and we had discussed getting away for a few days after our anniversary for just the two of us. We would use some of the vacation time as family time and at least a few days of alone time.

That was something we always did to keep our love fresh and exciting, having our alone time. We would get a babysitter or leave the kids with a family member or our parents so we could have our "special time." Sometimes it was a few days or just a weekend. It could be just a night away if that's all we could do. That was a priority for us, and it worked. Our love had remained passionate this long and showed no signs of slowing down or growing cold or even lukewarm. We wanted it to be *hot*!

Please don't take your spouse or significant other for granted. There are so many relationships I have seen diminish from lack of effort. If love is worth having, it's worth working at. If you take your significant other for granted, there may be someone else out there ready to snap them up or at least give them the attention you are not giving them. I think that is why the divorce rate is so high, and it's sad when you stop and think that at one time this couple was in love. They were passionate and intimate! What happened? Sometimes all it takes is a little effort, a little appreciation. It doesn't have to be something big. It can be as simple as a card or a note telling that special someone in your life that you love them and appreciate them. I can tell you from experience it is definitely worth the time and effort you put into it.

I started planning our ten-year anniversary four months in advance. I had arranged to take four days off from work and a weekend. We always loved getting away to the beach. Kris loved Daytona Beach, and she also loved St. Pete Beach. I made hotel reservations in both places. I arranged some time away during the evening to go shopping without her knowing it and purchased all new outfits and clothes for both of us for the trip. I got everything we would need for a week getaway, right down to her panties (those were fun picking out), hairbrush, toothbrush and toothpaste, shampoo, and all the other essentials. I didn't want to take anything from the house and have her get suspicious to my plan.

Kris would usually drive me to work in the morning, so she would have the car to drive herself and the kids to school. I arranged to have a rental car at work on that special day. I got dressed for work and had her drop me off just like any other day. I had packed our suitcases and had them at work the day before. I had arranged with the pastor and his wife to help in the process. On that day, Kris was going to be with the pastor's wife visiting a church member who had been sick and just out of the hospital. I changed clothes there at work and loaded everything in the rental car and swung by our house to get a few things that I couldn't sneak out, like her curling iron, hair dryer, etc. Then I drove to Mrs. Haynes's house, the church member they were visiting.

I pulled up to the house, went up to the door, and knocked. Kris didn't even recognize me at first. After all, this couldn't be Bill. She had just dropped him off at work in his work clothes. Who could this be pulling up in that Lincoln Town Car and fancy clothes?

She said, "Who is that? Oh my God, it's Bill! What are you doing here? What's going on?"

I told her, "It's our anniversary, and we are going away for a few days. I have everything taken care of. Your chariot awaits!"

Kris said, "How... what... ahh ... you couldn't have... Shawn, were you in on this?"

The pastor's wife said, "Yes, we were in on it from the start. You two go and have a great time. We will take care of everything here. Have fun!"

Kris said, "What about our clothes? I have stuff I need from the house. I have to pack some things."

I told her that it was all taken care of. All she had to do was put her pretty little self in the front seat and sit back for the ride. She couldn't believe it. She was speechless and smiling from ear to ear. Here was my beautiful wife caught totally off guard and surprised. She was absolutely radiant!

Mrs. Haynes and Shawn were excited too. They were happy to be a part of it. They said, "We're excited for you! Now you two run off and have fun!" I walked Kris to the car and let her in. She was full of questions. I told her that I would explain everything on the way.

"Right now, just sit back and enjoy the ride and we will get this adventure started." I drove out to the main road and asked, "You get to decide. Would you like to go to St. Pete Beach or Daytona?"

She said, "I have always kinda liked Daytona."

I said, "Daytona it is!" and turned left, heading toward the interstate.

During the course of the drive, I explained to her how I had gotten everything done and kept it a secret from her. How I was able to go shopping and get all the things we needed and how her mom, my mom, and the pastor and his wife were all in on it. I told her how I arranged for the time off and all the help I had from family, friends, and coworkers to pull this off.

She couldn't stop smiling. She was so cute. She said, "I can't believe you did all this and pulled this off right under my nose. How did you keep everything such a secret?"

I told her, "I had a lot of help, and I'm pretty good at making you happy."

She said, "Yes, you are!"

I said "Sweetheart, you are worth it. Just to see that beautiful smile makes it all worthwhile! I love you!"

We spent four glorious days and nights at Daytona Beach. It was like our second (or third, or sixth) honeymoon! At dinner on our anniversary I gave Kris a pearl necklace (a real one, get your mind out of the gutter!).

She loved it, and it looked great on her. On the last day of our getaway, we got up and went out on the beach and watched the sunrise over the Atlantic Ocean. We spent a great morning together, and then we packed up and headed back home. That evening we went out to St. Pete Beach and watched the sun set over the Gulf of Mexico. Both the sunrise and the sunset were absolutely beautiful and cloud free. With the sounds of the waves on the sandy shore and our arms wrapped around one another, we were so in love and just soaking up this awesome experience.

I believe this life is meant to be lived and shared with the ones you love. The memories you make during your short stay here in this beautiful place God has created are what is truly important. That is what you will remember as you get older. The experiences in your life are what make it worth living. This one was for me. It is a memory I will carry with me for the rest of my life. I can still see it like it was yesterday.

What memories do you have? What experiences do you keep in that special place in your heart and in your mind? Do you want more of them? It's not too late. As long as you have breath in your body and life and love in your heart, you can make some special memories that will warm your heart and keep you smiling.

Our tenth anniversary is a memory that will stay with me forever, and it's an experience that no one can take away!

Our love was still growing!

Chapter 11

Our Ups and Downs

IN ANY MARRIAGE, IN ANY RELATIONSHIP, there are going to be ups and downs, good times and bad times. We definitely had ours. The things I tend to remember, though, are the good times. That is what I *choose* to remember. Even with all the trials and tribulations in my life—and you will read about a lot more of them to come—I feel truly blessed. I think of myself as a truly blessed child of God. He has a reason for everything. Oftentimes we can't see what that reason is. That's where faith comes in. It's not always easy, and it may not seem right or even fair to you sometimes. God does have a plan though. Sometimes you just have to trust Him.

I have experienced love on so many different levels and so many different kinds of love. My love for Kris was incredible. My love for my children changed me from a drinking, drug-using, rowdy biker and bouncer to a loving father when two beautiful children who were needing me and showing me how to love. My love for my family and my love for my friends are two different types of love that I get to experience. Then there is my love for God and His love for me. Without His love, there is no way I could make it through this life and still have the positive outlook that I do.

The years from 1989 through 1998 were some years of ups and downs for us. I was working full time and trying to start several different businesses at the time and raise a family and be there for my kids. I always wanted to be the dad who was there for my kids when they were in activities at school or at church. I wanted them to know they were important and that I loved and supported each of them in whatever they did. For the most part, I did that. That's not to say I didn't make mistakes. I did. With five kids, there were bound to be times when we fell short. The funny thing is, these kids didn't come with an instruction manual. I always tried to do my best for them though.

One of the businesses we tried to start was an Amway business. This was probably my favorite. We didn't make much money at it and we didn't get to become Amway "Royalty," but we did get the chance to really work the business. Kris and I got to spend a lot of time together while building it. We got to travel together to different events and meetings and seminars. We learned a lot through the training part of that business that would help in other businesses later on. Also Amway was one of the few businesses that actually encourage you to put God first.

Kris and I loved being together no matter what we were doing. She was my best friend, my lover, and my soul mate all wrapped up in one beautiful package. When we were in Amway, we got to be together even more. They encourage couples to build the business together. Traveling to different meetings and Amway events was a great way for us to spend time together and get away from the everyday stresses of life. Raising five kids, working, church, and life in general can sometimes get to you. The traveling and the Amway events were a blessing to us. We got to get away for a bit and talk. We got to see new places and get away from the day-to-day rituals of our life and enjoy each other. We got to make love to each other in those new places and really enjoy being together. It helped us renew our love and appreciation for one another. We really enjoyed our Amway days.

As they say, life happens. Time marches on, and for several reasons, the Amway business went by the wayside. Between family, church, and job responsibilities, we just couldn't maintain them all, and something had to go. We just didn't have or better yet *make* the time to make it work. They will tell you while building that business that it works if you work it. As I said, though, we did learn a lot from it, and like anything else it is what *you* make of it. We had no regrets for doing the business and are better for having been a part of it.

Shortly after we left the Amway business, I was working for another automotive company and was involved in an incident that would change things for us, and not for the better either. I was working as the head technician for Montgomery Ward. I had a car on the alignment lift and had it raised in the air. When you release the air pressure on the lift, it is supposed to let the car down slowly. What I didn't know was that this lift had an air leak, so when I released the air pressure, the car dropped immediately and struck me in the back of the head, knocking me to the ground and unconscious. I woke up in the hospital the next day with a fractured neck and a concussion. Thank God it was only a Honda that fell on me and not a full-sized Chevy! I have always been kind of hard-headed anyway. Because of that incident, though, I was in the hospital for a week and out of work for six months.

I was still the sole supporter of our family, so this took quite a toll on our finances. I got workers' compensation, which was 60 percent of my salary. However, it didn't cover any of the commission I made. Over half of the money I made was based on commission and the jobs I sold and completed. This really hurt. We had savings, and it was being depleted at a rapid rate. After just a couple months, we began to feel the pinch pretty badly. We cut back every place we could. Spaghetti was a staple as dinner, and our kids grew sick of mac and cheese and Ramen noodles.

After a couple months, I felt better and felt I could go back to work. The doctor wouldn't sign off on it, though. He had me going to rehab twice a week, and even though I was doing everything and then some in the rehab, he still thought I needed more time to heal. In all reality, I couldn't do some of the things I used to do. The physical, financial, and emotional pressure started to weigh on our marriage. There were a lot of the extra things I'd always done that now fell on Kris. We seemed to be drifting apart. This was a low point for us.

I was getting stronger day by day and started to do some side work to make ends meet, but the bills were still piling up. I prayed about it and really didn't see an answer right away. The more I tried, the further things seemed to slip away. Tensions were riding high, and Kris and I weren't as passionate as we once had been. Then a wonderful idea came to me. I did a job for a customer and invested it in what I knew was the most important thing. I invested in our marriage. I took that money and surprised Kris with a night away in a hotel. It was just what the doctor ordered. We walked on the beach and talked. We took time and looked deeply into each other's eyes. We spent a night away and made mad, passionate love and rekindled our romance, our love, and our commitment to one another. What a great night! Our love grew again!

Shortly after that, I got an opportunity to take over a three-bay service station in downtown St. Pete. The guy who owned it needed someone to run it and offered it to me. I told him I didn't have the money for the rent or the inventory and equipment, and he said to just come and work it and we would figure it out. So I did. The doctor still didn't want to release me, but I couldn't pass up this opportunity. There was a mechanic working at the shop already, and he became my mechanic and did the work. I just supervised and diagnosed and sold the work. By the time the doctor released me, I had built that business into a thriving garage and had started paying for the rent and the inventory. Things were back on track.

The shop was succeeding, and our kids were doing well in school. We started looking for a house to buy. We were able to help our kids out.

Nick got a job with a traveling salesman from our church and got married to his high school sweetheart, Dulcie. Kerstin took a trip to Germany, where she met her husband, Sean, who was stationed in the air force over there. Our family was transitioning and expanding in a whole new way. Yes, things were going well and did for several years. I ran that shop for over four years, and we did very well.

The owner of the service station saw how successful it had become and wanted more money for rent. At first this was not a problem. We had a verbal agreement on the amount of the rent.However, we were doing much better than expected, so I was willing to share the benefits of our success. He was an Egyptian and spent four months a year in Egypt. Then he raised the rent again in a month. Altogether he tried to raise the rent six times in six months. I tried to talk to him about it, but he wouldn't listen to reason. He used the increased rent to pay for his trip to Egypt. I was a bit too trusting in business but learned pretty quickly that a verbal contract isn't worth the paper it is *not* written on.

Kris and I discussed what to do next, and we decided we would step out on faith and close that shop and search for another opportunity. We knew God had something better in store for us. I bought and sold a few cars, and the bills got paid. It was Christmastime, and we had already gotten everything done for the holidays. I took a month off and enjoyed my family for the holidays that year. We spent time together, and during one of our nights out, I spotted a shop that was six blocks away from the service station that was just going on the market. The next day I talked to the owner and signed the papers, and Five Star Automotive was born. It was named Five Star because there was one star for each of my children.

I was able to retain over 70 percent of the clients from the service station, which gave us a great start. The business took off and was even more successful than the service station had been. This was a down that, through faith and love, turned into an up. It became a family business, and Nick wound up being my manager in that shop.

Through the love and commitment Kris and I had for each other, we were able to come through all of our ups and downs together. We came through even stronger and more in love than we'd been when we started. It wasn't always easy. Great things rarely are. As I said, life happens. Things won't always go the way you want them to. One thing I have learned is that love and marriage take time, dedication, and work—at least if you want to have a good (or great) one. It is definitely worth it though. To get a love that lasts a lifetime is *definitely* worth the effort. The rewards are awesome!

Love—true love–makes the world go round

Chapter 12

Twenty Years and Going Stronger Than Ever

DO YOU WANT A GREAT MARRIAGE? DO YOU
want to know how it feels to have a love others only dream about? Then
take time for the ones you love. Let them know how you feel. Show
them once in a while with the little things. Buy her some flowers on a
Tuesday just because. Tell your significant other that you love him or
her often. Let him or her know how you feel. Don't just say, "Oh, I told
them once. They should know." Your significant other needs to know
you still love him or her and find him or her attractive. Buy her a teddy
bear (or a teddy for her to wear) once in a while. Little unexpected things
can make all the difference. It can turn a lukewarm relationship into a
burning, passionate one. Isn't your marriage or relationship worth it? I
know mine is!

I really enjoyed doing that kind of thing. I would buy a Tuesday
present one in a while. Try sending a card in the mail just to say you love
them—not for an anniversary or a birthday (don't forget those either
though) but "just because I was thinking of you." It doesn't have to be a
big thing or all the time. When you do this, it just lets her or him know
that he or she is still special, still loved, and still important to you. Try

it and see if it works for you. I know it did for me. I learned to do this, and we had a long and very happy life together. The intimacy and the sex were great too! That could be a book all in itself (maybe my next one).

The bottom line is that if your love and your marriage are worth doing, then it's worth doing right. No two people or couples are the same. Try different things and learn what works for you. Make it fun and exciting. We did, and we loved it!

We had made it to twenty years of marriage, and we were more in love than ever! It's a wonderful feeling to know that your wife is also your lover and your best friend. One thought that did come to my mind was, *What am I going to do to top the tenth anniversary?* So I began to think about it and develop a plan. I might not be able to pull off the total surprise of number ten, but because of our businesses I was now in a position to do it with more style and try to make it even more over the top. She knew I would be planning something. She just didn't know what. This time I got my mother as an accomplice.

Kris knew I was up to something and said, "What are you planning?"

I said, "Don't you worry about what I'm planning. You will find out soon enough. This time I want you to go shopping and get yourself ready for it."

I told her that she and my mom needed to spend a few days shopping and get some new clothes, enough for five days, a new bathing suit, and a nice dress for dinner one evening. I would take care of the rest. She was so excited, and they had a great time shopping and trying to figure out just what I might have planned this time. Neither one knew what it was I was up to. All they knew was that I was planning a fabulous twentieth anniversary, and if the ten year was that good, this one could be even better.

I had been in the planning stage for several months. I already had my clothes bought and my suitcase packed. I kept it hidden at the shop. I also had a surprise picked out for her. When we first got married, I couldn't afford much in the way of wedding rings. They were pretty small and not very expensive. After all, we were just getting started in life back then and had to pay for everything ourselves for the wedding. They served their purpose all these years though. With our big day coming, I had ordered a new set of wedding rings for us. I picked out the design and the setting of the engagement and wedding rings then picked out the diamonds to go in them.

I also had a special night planned. I told her to be ready on June 10, 1998, by four o'clock with her suitcase packed and ready to go. I had reserved a limo for the evening and had the driver pick us up at our home. Shortly before four o'clock, I came home from the shop and got myself ready, and we got the evening started. One of the things we did when we were dating was go to Tampa Jai Ali. We would go to watch the games and bet on the teams, so that evening that's where we started. It just happened to be one of the last nights that Tampa Jai Ali would be there. They were closing their doors forever. It was perfect timing for us. After we stayed there for a while, I had the limo driver take us to Bern's Steak House in Tampa. Bern's is one of the best steakhouses in the country. I had made reservations for seven o'clock.

We had a wonderful dinner, and I made us reservations for the dessert room for after dinner. Just as we finished dinner and before going to the dessert room, I retrieved the rings out of my pocket. I then took Kris by the hand, looked into her eyes, got down on one knee, and said, "Kris, would you marry me again?" as I opened the box with the new rings.

Kris turned red, got the biggest smile on her face, and yelled, "*Yes! Yes I will! I love you, Bill!*" Then I got up from my knee and pulled her into me. We hugged and kissed deeply right there in the middle of the room. The waiter saw what happened, and the room broke out in applause.

He said, "Did you just do what I think you did?" I told him what was going on, that it was our twentieth anniversary, and that she said she would still marry me even after all these years!

After we had dessert, we left, and I had already told the limo driver to take us for a long drive down the beach starting at Clearwater Beach and heading south. The last time we went to Daytona.This time it would be St. Pete Beach. She didn't have a clue where we were going, and she really didn't care at this point. She just knew that we were in love, and whatever we did, it would be special. After a long drive down the beach, the limo driver pulled up to the Don Cesar, a luxury hotel on St. Pete Beach, where I had made reservations. I had champagne and strawberries waiting in the room. It was a glorious night. We didn't even come out of the room for two days. Room service was our lifeline. We spent five fabulous days there at the Don Cesar and enjoyed every moment of it. The hotel is right on the beautiful white sand beach on the Gulf of Mexico. The grounds there are spectacular and beutifully landscaped, with tropical flowers and foliage.

After the fourth day, Kris said."Bill, is there any way we coud spend another day or two here? I am just having such a good time."

Kris very rarely asked for anything like that. I imediately got on the phone to the front desk and took care of it. She called her sister and our daughters and had them come out one of the days to see the beach and this wonderful hotel property.

Twenty years in marriage together. All the ups and downs and all the things we had been through, and we were still so deeply in love. We were still best friends. Our love was stronger than ever, and we were still passionate about each other.

It's hard to believe but even after twenty years together…

our love blossomed even more!

Chapter 13

Disaster Strikes

YOU NEVER KNOW WHAT TOMORROW MAY bring. We are not guaranteed we will even have a tomorrow. That is why we should try to live our lives for today. Enjoy each moment you have here on this beautiful earth that God has created for us. Try to enjoy all the things and people in your life because tomorrow they may be gone. If you love someone, make sure they know it. Tell them often how you feel. Let people know that you appreciate them. Live with no regrets if you can. Things in this life can change in an instant. The people you love today can be gone tomorrow.

Things were going very well for Kris and me. Our shop was doing great. We'd done a lot of remodeling around the house and made it the way we wanted it, painting inside and out and redoing the pool and patio areas. I had a good crew at the shop, so I started taking Monday afternoons off just for Kris and me to spend quality time together. I had Nick as my manager, and he was doing a terrific job. I would go in to the shop on Monday mornings and get things going, and then at about noon or one o'clock, I would take off.

Kris and I would go to lunch or go to the beach. Sometimes we would go to a movie or go shopping. It became our special date day. The kids were older now. Nick, Kerstin, and Jeremy were out of the house starting families of their own. Anita and Rebecca were in school on Monday afternoons and had things to do there and were involved in extracurricular activities.

We loved spending time together. We always had. Now we were just getting to do more of it. Besides being my wife and my lover, Kris was my best friend. Imagine that—a wife, lover, confidante, and best friend all rolled into one! I was a very blessed man! We talked about everything together. We talked of our past and how far we had come. We talked about how things were going now and how we felt about each other. We realized how blessed we were. We also talked about the future and where we saw our lives going and how we would handle unforeseen events that could come upon us. We discussed what would happen if one of us should pass away suddenly and the other was left here to go on. We both agreed that the other should go on and remarry. Neither of us wanted the other to go on alone. We talked about what we wanted our funerals to be like. Kris expressed that she wanted to be cremated.

She said, "Ashes to ashes is what the Bible says, so that's what I want."

For some reason Kris started talking more and more about her dying before me. She said she had a strong feeling about it. I tried to reassure her that we had a long and happy life ahead of us. She still seemed to have that feeling though and expressed it every so often.

One night we were talking before bed, and she said, "You know, I'm going to die before you. I don't want you to be sad for me, because we both know I'll be in heaven."

I said, "Cut it out. You know we have a lifetime together yet."

Kris, said "No, I don't think it will be that long. I want you to be happy and remarry right away. As a matter of fact, you're going to meet a blond-haired, blue-eyed bombshell who you're going to fall madly in love with." Then she paused for a moment and looked at me with her sexy little smile and said, "But you can't have too much fun with her!"

We both laughed, and I told her to stop talking like that and tried to reassure her we were going to grow old together. That was in February of 2000.

On April 23, 2000, it was Easter Sunday morning. I woke up, and Kris wasn't in bed with me. This happened from time to time because she sometimes had trouble sleeping. She would get up and go into the family room and watch TV or go out by the pool and sit outside. I got up that morning and went looking for her. I looked through the house and called for her, but there was no answer. I then went to the sliding glass doors that led out back to the pool area. I opened the door and stepped outside. When I looked toward the pool, I saw Kris floating facedown in the middle. Immediately I screamed at the top of my lungs for Rebecca to call 911 and jumped into the water! I grabbed Kris and turned her over and saw that she was already turned blue. She was stiff, and it was apparent that she had been in there for some time. I began to cry and scream out loud, and I just lost it! I got her to the side of the pool and lifted her out of the water and onto the deck.

I was crying out, "No, Kris, *no!* This can't be happening!" Becca came to the back door with the phone and saw her mom lying there and began to cry and scream out as well. She ran to where we were and saw what I saw—that Kris was dead.

I couldn't believe it. After all it was just a few hours ago that she was so alive, so vibrant, and we were so happy. Now here she was, lying on the deck of our pool lifeless, stiff, and blue. Her spirit had left her, and now her body seemed to be a lifeless shell. To say I was devastated would be an understatement. I had just lost my wife, my lover, and my best friend. I had just lost my soul mate and the love of my life. The woman who made my life worth living was gone.

When things like this happen, it seems to either bring out the best or the worst in families and friends. It brought out the best with ours. All my children rallied together. Naturally all of us were grieving and devastated by our loss. However, they all came together and stepped up to do what needed to be done. Kerstin flew in from Texas, where she and her family were living, and helped me with the arrangements. Nick stepped up and handled everything at the shop. Jeremy was instrumental in dealing with friends and family and letting people know what had happened. Anita and Rebecca were there to support me and each other in this time of grief. Kris's sisters came and were so awesome and supportive, as was my mom and the rest of my family. Friends and neighbors helped out, sending condolences and bringing dinners for us all. We didn't have much of an appetite, but having it there was a great help and much appreciated. It was by far the most difficult thing we had ever been faced with as a family.

We had the service at a funeral home in Gulfport. One of my clients owned the place and helped out with the arrangements. After the service, we all came back to the house. Kerstin had purchased a big package of those votive candles that are made to float on the water. Just as it was getting dark, we each lit a candle and put it in the pool to float. We had discussed what we were going to do with the pool now that Kris was gone. Should we keep it? Should we fill it in and make a larger backyard? The kids and I talked about it and agreed that she would want us to keep it and enjoy it. She loved the pool and the backyard. How could we do that now though? With what had just happened, I didn't think I would want to be doing anything in that pool.

After all the candles were lit, we all gathered around the pool in a circle. Family, friends, and neighbors were just standing there holding hands looking at the pool and the candles, no one really knowing what to do or say next. All of a sudden, I looked at Kerstin, and she got a mischievous little grin on her face and jumped into the pool! Then Becca jumped in. Then some of the kids and cousins who were there followed suit and leaped into the pool! Before you knew it, everyone was in the water swimming and splashing around and laughing. Grown adults and kids alike were frolicking in the water, fully clothed, just come from a memorial service and having a grand old time. It was just what the doctor ordered. It was exactly what Kris would have wanted. I'm sure she was looking down and laughing right along with us.

Over the next few weeks, we all tried to get back to living a somewhat normal life. We did the best we could anyway, without Kris there. I was back at the shop, although Nick was pretty much still running things. Thank God! Kerstin was there for a while and then went back to Texas. Jeremy got back to his business and his family. Anita and Rebecca got back to school. We all tried to do what we knew Kris would have wanted us to do, which was to go on living. When I was at home alone, though, it was like I could still feel her there.

This next part I don't think I have ever told anyone. It is about an experience I had a couple weeks after Kris died. Sometimes when I was home by myself, I still talked to her as if she was still there. It may sound strange and some people may think I'm crazy or making things up, but I know what I felt. I know the experience that I had, and it was so wonderful that I had to include it in this book.

One evening I was home alone. The girls were out with friends or something, so I was there by myself and sitting at the computer. I was missing Kris so much. I started talking to her out loud and telling her how much I loved her and missed her. I was crying and expressing my feelings for my wife and lover. Suddenly, an awe-inspiring feeling came over me. I felt Kris's presence, and it consumed my whole body. It was an overwhelming feeling of love. I have never felt anything like it before or since. It was like Kris came down and permeated my very soul with her magnificent and never-ending love. It filled every part of my being.

It was like a glimpse of what heaven must feel like. I just sat there unable to move and enjoyed every second of it. The sensation lasted about fifteen or twenty minutes. I can still remember the splendor of that time. It is something that I will never forget, and the effects of those moments will last a lifetime!

Love—true love—is really never ending!

Chapter 14

A New Beginning (the Blond-Haired, Blue-Eyed Bombshell)

SEVERAL MONTHS HAD PASSED SINCE KRIS had died, and life seemed to be going on. The sky hadn't fallen, and the world was still going on for most people. I was extremely lonely though. Kris and I were together for almost twenty-four years. We shared everything with each other and were rarely apart. The intimacy, friendship, companionship, romance, and sex were all gone. Kris wanted me to go on, and I knew that. She wanted me to be happy and find love again. That was easier said than done though. After all, Kris was all I knew as a lover and a soul mate for almost a quarter of a century. We were together for over half of my life. The thought of me starting over seemed very daunting.

I talked with several members of my family and a few friends about the possibility of me starting to date. They all thought it was a good idea and expressed the fact that Kris would have wanted me to. A couple of them even said Kris mentioned that to them before she died. After all, she was gone and wasn't coming back. I would see her one day again in heaven, but for now I had to go on. So with much trepidation, I decided I would give it a try.

I dated a few women that friends or family hooked me up with and didn't feel a real connection with any of them. I tried a dating site and went on a few dates with ladies I had met on there. None of them were right, and I could tell. Still I kept trying. I would sometimes go on a date once or twice a week. Other times it would be a while between dates.

One evening I was meeting a woman who I'd met online for dinner. I had picked a restaurant I liked and was meeting her there. The restaurant was in a strip mall on Park Street in St. Petersburg. I got there a little early and parked next to the restaurant in front of a tanning and nail salon. Standing in the doorway of the salon were two beautiful blondes. They were both drop-dead gorgeous! I thought to myself, *How can I get to meet these two lovely ladies?* I saw the large neon sign in the window and got an idea. I got out of my truck and walked up to them and said, "Do you do nails here?"

They looked at the large glowing neon sign that said "Nails" and then looked back at me and Diane said, "Ah, yes."

I said, "Good, I've been looking for a new place to get my daughters' nails done."

That broke the ice and began the conversation. As it turned out, they were twin sisters. They were fraternal twins and not identical. Debbie was the outgoing and flamboyant one, and Diane was a bit more subdued and shy. Debbie was full of questions and was asking about my daughters and where I worked and where they got their nails done before and so on.

Then she said, "So where is your wife?"

I explained that my wife had passed away and I was raising my daughters on my own now. At first they thought I was just saying that as a pick-up line and thought that I was probably still married. Debbie thought, *Now I've heard them all!* This is what they told me later. Being two single and beautiful twins, they had heard all kinds of pick-up lines.

They thought that this one took the cake though. Before the conversation was over, things were explained, and I had set up an appointment to bring in Rebecca to get her nails done that week. I also knew it was Diane who I wanted to ask on a date.

I really did take the girls to get their nails done from time to time. It worked out well for me that I got to have them done in this particular nail salon. On the day I took Becca to get her nails done, Debbie had an eye exam and they dilated her eyes, and she couldn't see correctly to do her nails and botched the job. Diane didn't do nails, so she couldn't help. They apologized and set up another time so they could redo Becca's nails at no charge.

We came back in a couple days, and Debbie was going to do Rebecca's nails again. This time Debbie's doctor had switched her medication, and she was having a bad reaction. Her vision was off, and she was feeling dizzy. Debbie still tried, but she botched the job again. Diane had to leave early to pick up her son, so she couldn't help.

By this time Rebecca knew what was going on, and she said, "Just ask her on a date, Dad. Don't use me as a reason to come in here."

Debbie thought I was interested in her and started to tell me that I wasn't her type. She liked guys with long hair and rock and roll band type guys. I said, "Well I'm actually interested in your sister, Diane."

She said, "Oh, well you're just her type!"

The next evening, I came back by the salon, and Diane was there by herself. It was late November, and I thought I would use the excuse of buying gift certificates for the tanning salon as Christmas gifts that year. What a novel idea. Where would I ever get an idea like that? I walked in and asked Diane about the certificates and she didn't know where they were, so she called Debbie. She said they were in the desk. Diane rummaged through the desk but still couldn't find them. She was nervous because Debbie had told her that I liked her and might ask her out. I was nervous too because I was using all kinds of excuses to go by and see her and still hadn't asked her out. Finally she found them, and I purchased four of them.

Then I said, "How would you like to have dinner with me one even—"

Before I even finished the sentence, she said, "*Yes!*" with a big, happy smile on her face. We made plans to meet that Wednesday for dinner and a comedy show. I was going to pick her up at the salon.

Diane was a single mom. She had never been married. Her son was the result of a long-term relationship she'd had with his father. She'd had a couple relationships over the years but never wanted to marry any of them. She thought that she'd never get married. We dated for a while, and after a short time we became an exclusive couple, and neither of us dated anyone else. We went through the holidays and the New Year, and Diane told me that she had fallen in love with me. She knew that I was the one she wanted to be with for the rest of her life. I was a bit taken aback. I was starting to feel the same way about her, but I was also feeling conflicted about it. After all, I had just lost the love of my life, my best friend, and my soul mate less than a year before. How could I be feeling this way so quickly? I felt guilty for feeling the way I did. I couldn't help it though. Diane was so beautiful inside and out. She had a great big heart and loved kids and animals. To me she was absolutely gorgeous. Now here she was expressing that she loved me and wanted to be with me for the rest of her life.

We continued dating for several more months. In May Diane got a bonus check and wanted to treat me to a four-day cruise. I was really hard to convince. As soon as she asked, I said, "Okay! When do we leave?"

We sailed from Miami to Key West and then to Cozumel. It was a wonderful cruise and a great chance for both of us to get away and have some alone time. Each of us being single parents, we didn't get much of that, and that was fine. I love being a dad, and she loved being a mom.

Sometimes you just need to get away and recharge your batteries. What better way than on a Caribbean cruise?

We saw the sights and did some shopping in Key West and Cozumel. We stopped in a jewelry store called Diamonds International and started looking at things. We looked at bracelets, necklaces, and rings. We looked at different rings, and for some reason, I didn't like the diamonds they had in the settings.

The manager said, "Oh, señor, we can change the diamond for you." Then he took us in the back, and we started looking at diamonds.

I saw a couple I liked, and then I told him "These are nice. When we get ready I will come back and pick something out."We left that room and returned to the showroom. Something came over me right then and there. I knew the exact diamond and the exact setting that I wanted, and I knew I wanted to marry Diane.

She was looking at necklaces in one of the displays, and I excused myself and went to the back of the store to talk to the manager. I told him which diamond I wanted and what ring and setting I wanted and asked him how long it would take him to get it done. We were leaving in a couple hours, and I wanted to have it done before we left. He assured me they would get it done and suggested we go upstairs to a restaurant and have a long, leisurely lunch. He would have the ring ready when we came back. I told him we would, and I took Diane upstairs for lunch.

We went to the restaurant, and we were talking about our trip and the things we had seen in the store and what we were going to be doing when we got back home. We both agreed that we were having an awesome time and didn't want it to end.

After lunch I said, "Let's walk back through that jewelry store one more time. There's something I want to see."

She said, "Okay."

We walked downstairs and went back into the store. I caught the manager's eye, and he nodded. I walked over to him, and he showed me the ring and handed it to me without Diane seeing it. I turned around, took Diane by the hand, and dropped down to one knee. I looked her in the eyes and said, "Diane, will you marry me?"

I thought she was going to explode with excitement. She had the biggest smile break out across her pretty face as she yelled, "Yes! Yes, I'll marry you!"

I placed that custom ring on her finger and got up, and we kissed and hugged each other. The entire store broke out in applause and cheers. I couldn't believe it! We were engaged! I didn't plan for this to happen. She didn't expect this to happen. It just seemed so right. Everything fell into place so perfectly. We walked out of that store as a newly engaged couple. She was still smiling from ear to ear and staring at her ring. We then got in a taxi to go back to the ship.

On the way she said, "Let's stop at Carlos and Charley's to toast our engagement."

I said "Sure, why not?"

We got there and ordered two shots of tequila to celebrate. Just then she looked down and said, "Oh no, my purse!"

Her purse was missing. In all the excitement she wasn't paying attention and thought she must have left it in the cab. We had to get that purse. All her stuff was in there. Her credit cards—her social security card, her driver's license, and her ship ID. She couldn't get back on the ship without it! I looked at my watch and saw that we had one hour to find it and get back to the ship before it sailed.

We went outside to hail a cab, and suddenly we noticed that *all* the cabs looked exactly alike! They were all red cabs with white tops. They were almost all the same make and model of car. How were we going to find that one cab in this sea of cabs and do it in less than an hour? I got one of the cabs to stop and explained the situation to the driver. He got on the radio and told the dispatcher of our dilemma. We thought we were really screwed. We didn't think there was any way we were going to find the purse and make it back to the ship in time.

Just then the cabbie came to us and said, "Señor, the man with your purse is bringing it to the cab stand. It's just a few blocks away."

We were overjoyed and relieved. The driver took us to their cab stand where we were to meet the other driver who was bringing her purse back. We got there, and he was waiting for us. We got the purse and paid and tipped the driver.

He didn't want to accept the tip and said, "Oh, señor, this is too much. I was just doing the right thing."

We assured him that it was well worth it to us and that we appreciated his honesty. We then asked him to take us back to the ship. He said, "Of course, señor, my pleasure."

We made it back to the ship with five minutes to spare. What a ride! What a trip! That is one I will never forget. It was quite an adventure.

Love has a way of making things work out. At least it has for me. It took a heartbroken widower back to knowing the love of a very special lady. It turned a lonely, jaded single mom who thought *marriage* was a dirty word into a blushing, smiling, and beautiful bride. On September 27, 2002, Diane Pamela Morton walked down the aisle of a small church in Seminole, Florida, to become Diane Pamela Kyne. It was on that day I married my blond-haired, blue-eyed bombshell.

Love wins again!

(Sorry, Kris. I did have a lot of fun with her.)

Chapter 15

Blending Families and Changing Plans

WE TOOK ANOTHER CRUISE FOR OUR honeymoon. Diane had always wanted to ride horses on the beach. That was one of her dreams. We got to do that in Jamaica, along with climbing the Dunn River waterfall. One of my dreams was to swim with dolphins, and we did that on our honeymoon as well. We spent a wonderful seven days away at sea to celebrate our love and our marriage. Our life together was just beginning, and we were so happy. Diane and I made sure we cherished every moment of it. We were off to a fantastic start as a married couple.

When we came back home, it was time to get back to real life and start to blend our two families together. Diane and her son, Kevin, came to live with me and my two daughters, Anita and Rebecca, who were still home with me. Our house was a four-bedroom home, so each of the kids had their own room. It was a split plan, so Diane and I had our privacy on the other side of the house. All of our children got along well most of the time. As it can be with any major changes in a family dynamic, there were little issues and disagreements that came up from time to time. Kevin, being an only child all his life, had some difficulty sharing—sharing anything. My girls weren't always angels either, and they could be a pain in the butt sometimes.

In most of my marriage to Kris, God was a big part, and I know He is what helped us through a lot of what we went through. His love is something that you can't really explain. You just have to experience it. Near the end of her life, we weren't going to church and were not close to God as a family. It was my fault that we drifted away from the church and from a close relationship with Him, and I take full responsibility for that. I was the leader of the house, and I allowed us to fall away from God as a family. I have often thought maybe that was why God let Kris die. In my heart I know that isn't the reason, but when something like that happens, I think it is only natural to look for an explanation or for someone or something to blame.

Here I was now with a second chance at love—a love that was amazing and so mutually real for each of us, and we felt so blessed to have found each other. Diane was a Christian, and we did go to church once in a while. It was not like Kris and I did, but I figured showing up once a month was good enough for a start. Once again though, I let life get in the way. I was so busy running my business and keeping up with our home and our newly blended family that I just didn't make God a priority like I should have. I can see that now, and looking back, I feel that would have been the right thing to do. Like they say, hindsight is 20/20.

One thing I did do, though, was let Diane know I loved her often. We would have our nights out and would get away by ourselves from time to time. It was kind of like what Kris and I did, only at this stage of my life I was able to do it a bit more often and in a bit more style. I would send her a card in the mail once in a while just to say I love you. There were times when I would leave little notes lying around for her to find or taped to the bathroom mirror for her to see first thing in the morning. Occasionally I would send her flowers for no particular reason or buy her a Tuesday present just because. I loved doing stuff like that. I had loved doing it with Kris, and I was continuing it with Diane.

When love is worth having, it is worth the effort it takes to make each other feel special, to feel loved. Don't just say as so many do, "Oh, I told them I loved them once. They should know."

No! Get off your butt, get a romantic bone in your body, and do something for that special someone in your life! It doesn't have to be something big or extravagant. It could be a single rose or a teddy bear or a card. Do something to let them know that you love them enough to put a little thought and effort into making them feel like the most important part of your life. I know I've said this stuff several times in this book, but damn it, it's *that*important, and it bears repeating! Let me tell you, it is well worth it. I know from personal experience that it is definitely the best investment you can make into your relationship. It can make an average marriage into one that others can only dream about.

Our love wasn't just a one-way street though. Diane took care of me too. Our love life was amazing, and she was very attentive in a lot of other ways as well. When I was out mowing the lawn or taking care of the pool, she would come out with a cold bottle of water and a cool towel for me. She would make sure I got enough rest and down time and would often have special snacks made for me when I was watching football or NASCAR. There were times when she knew I was in need of clothes or shoes and would either go shopping and get them or order them online so I would have the things I needed. Diane paid attention and knew what I liked, and I paid attention to her and knew what she liked. We really complemented each other like that. I would often pick out her clothes, and she would often pick out mine. After all, she got the benefit of seeing me in my clothes and I got the benefit of seeing Diane in (and out of) hers. Why not get what we each liked to see the other in?

It seemed like the longer we were together, the more our love grew for one another. It doesn't seem possible that you can love a person any more sometimes and then all of a sudden you do. Your love grows. Like with Kris, Diane and I had also become best friends. There is a unique bond that forms between a husband and wife when they go beyond being just lovers to becoming best friends. There is a level of trust and connection that I can't really explain except to say that the Bible is right. It says that a man shall leave his father and mother and cleave to his wife and they shall become one flesh. That is exactly how we felt, as if we were both one. That doesn't mean that we agreed on everything and that our entire life was just roses and daffodils. We had our own personalities and likes, dislikes, and preferences. However, we could almost always talk about things and reach an agreement on most everything.

Diane loved animals, and she had a few dogs when we met. She loved puppies especially. One of her passions was to breed Yorkshire Terriers. She had a female Yorkie, and we bred her several times. Diane really enjoyed taking care of the puppies. She had a hard time selling them after watching the puppies grow. Because she loved animals so much and had such a tender heart, it would also really get to her when something went wrong with one of the births. Inevitably there would be times when a puppy didn't make it, and Diane would take it very hard. I finally convinced her to stop breeding for that reason. I couldn't stand to see her get her heartbroken when she lost a puppy or had to sell them. She would get so attached and emotionally involved with each litter. To get her mind off breeding, I wound up buying her a macaw with an extremely large cage and a goat. She was always around birds as her mother had macaws and she had always wanted a goat for some reason. We got her a Nigerian dwarf goat, and I turned our side yard into a barnyard to accommodate it.

One of the things we loved to do together was to ride motorcycles. And because she got the animals she wanted, I got the motorcycle I wanted. She never thought she would enjoy riding until she rode with me. After the first couple of times she loved it almost as much as I did.

We would go for long rides on the weekends and were always signing up for and going on different organized rides in our area. Being in Florida, the weather was nice most of the time, and that gave us all the more time to ride. One of our favorite things to do was to ride up the beach and stop for lunch or dinner somewhere on the way. We would go for very long rides, and she got so comfortable riding that there were times when she actually fell asleep on the back. I had a Harley Ultra Classic with a large rear seat and padded wraparound backrest so she stayed comfortable and safe.

One of the other things we loved to do together was travel. We got to do quite a bit of that over the years. We would typically take two vacations a year and travel somewhere. We would go on a cruise or visit family in other states or just take a road trip some place we hadn't been. We loved spending time together on the road. Quite often Diane and I would take a short weekend trip somewhere in the state. It could be to Daytona where we would go for the races or Ft. Lauderdale or Miami. We even took the dogs sometimes and had car seats and a stroller for them. Diane had gotten them credentialed as service dogs with the paperwork and the vests, so we could take them anywhere with us.

Our love for one another was incredible. We took care of each other in all ways. She enjoyed taking care of me, and I loved taking care of her. I believe that our communication with one another was crucial in how our love blossomed. We would often talk of the dreams we had, the places we wanted to go and see, and what we wanted our lives to become. We talked about what we wanted to do when our kids were grown and out on their own. We even started looking for our dream home and discussed the type of house it should be and the location we wanted it in. We wanted a place close enough to the city and the beaches yet far enough away that we could have a large property and not be too close to neighbors.

I had planned to semi-retire from the shop and transition into real estate. I had dabbled in real estate over the years and enjoyed it. There were times when I would study the trends and made a few very lucrative deals. Nick was very capable of running the shop himself by this time, and the plan was to sell him the business and have the revenues pay for it. The shop had been going strong for many years, and we had a large and loyal client base. With both of these incomes, Diane and I could do the things we wanted to do and have the time to do them. That was the plan anyway. As often happens, though, life can throw you a curveball, and the best laid plans have to be adjusted.

The shop building I had purchased years ago was an old building that had been built in 1904, I was told. I had done some renovations to it and had updated the electrical system in the main shop. Every once in a while, we would smell something funny while we were in the office, and it smelled like burning plastic. One of my clients was an electrical contractor, and I asked him if he would send a technician over to check things out for me during the week as we were closed on the weekends. His guy came out and did a full inspection of the shop and the office areas. He told me that the shop area was fine and that the work that was done was more than adequate to handle the electrical load of all our shop equipment. The office, however, was another matter. The wiring in the office was the original wiring from the early 1900s and needed updating. I asked him how soon we would need to get it done and asked if it could wait for a couple months.

He told me it could, and then he said, "One thing you don't have to worry about is the building burning down on you."

That was on Wednesday. The following Saturday, I got a call at home that my shop was on fire! By the time I arrived, the place was totally engulfed in flames and the shop was almost a total loss. The fire department was on the scene and did all they could, but between the age of the building and some of the chemicals inside, there wasn't much they could do but contain the fire and keep it from spreading to the adjacent buildings.

As it had been in other tragedies in our life, our family and friends rallied together and pitched in to help. That's what families do—families that love each other anyway—and I have been very blessed with an amazing and very loving and supportive family. From my wife to my kids and brothers, sisters-in-law, nieces, nephews, cousins, and friends, everyone dove right in and helped where they could. We salvaged what we could, and I decided not to rebuild. I had already decided to step away from the shop and semi-retire. This just pushed up that date by about a year. I wound up selling the shop as it was and letting the new owners decide what they wanted to make of it.

In this life you just never know what tomorrow may hold in store for you. The Bible tells us not to think of what tomorrow may bring and to set our sights on today, on what is right here in front of us. Having gone through all the things that I had up to this point in my life there is no way I would have made it without all the love I had been blessed with over the years. First and foremost, I had God's love. His word says His grace is sufficient for us. I also had the love of my family and friends. When you go through hard times, you really learn who you can count on and who is there for you when the chips are down and the going gets tough. I have found that my close family and friends are all very special and loving people. Then there is the love of my wife (or in my case wives). The love we shared could be overwhelming sometimes and has always been such a blessing in times like these. The love that I shared with those two fabulous women was absolutely amazing! I am a very fortunate man! That is the way I *choose* to look at it.

Love overcomes even in the tough times!

Chapter 16

Love Taken Too Soon!

AFTER THE FIRE AND OUR DECISION NOT TO rebuild the shop, I went into real estate full time. I had gone to Sarasota to take some classes in real estate and learned different techniques to make deals work. I have tried most of them over the years. I have done everything from buying properties with no money down to paying cash at deep discounts to buying foreclosures and tax deed sales. I have bought properties on the courthouse steps and at auctions and even bought and sold properties on the same day using little or none of my own money. After a while, though, I focused mainly on buying foreclosed single-family properties and then fixing them up and flipping them. That was the option that I enjoyed the most and made the best return on investment. I enjoyed the challenge of finding the worst house in a good area and turning it into the nicest place in that neighborhood.

Diane and I had continued to look at properties in different areas that would be our next home. We search in the surrounding counties where the homes had more land than the homes in Pinellas County did. We tried Hernando County where my brother lived, but it seemed to be too far from the things we enjoyed doing, like going to the beach, good restaurants, theater, shopping, and too far from the airport. We also looked in Pasco County, which was just north of us. We liked some of the areas, but each time we would research a property, we would find something we didn't like about the home or the area.

Finally I found an area that was perfect. It was a place in Wesley Chapel in Pasco County that I came upon while looking at an investment property. The community had a country club, and all of the homes had at least an acre of land. That was a requirement to be able to build a house there. It was close enough to the city that we could get to any place we wanted to go relatively quickly and far enough out to be very private. As a matter of fact, there were even deer that would roam through the streets of the neighborhood on occasion. The property we found had a house and a large garage on one lot and an acre lot next to it. We were going to live in the existing house and build our dream home next door. We thought that once our home was built, we could use the existing home and garage for our businesses and storage. Diane had started an eBay business selling figurines and collectables. I could use the large garage for restoring cars and motorcycles and storing construction supplies for my real estate business.

At that time Kevin was living with us, as were my son Jeremy and his family. Jeremy had fallen on hard times, and Diane and I were helping him and his family get back on their feet by giving them a place to stay until they could save enough money to get places of their own. We told all of them of our plans to move and told them they had six months to get things together and move on. Jeremy assured me that six months would be plenty of time and thanked us for helping them out. Kevin, on the other hand, was another story. We had problems with him many times in the past. The police were called to our home for issues we had with him. He was arrested for criminal mischief, battery on law enforcement, resisting arrest, and possession of drugs. He also refused to leave our home when he was asked. One time when he was twenty-one, we even had to have him legally evicted because of his drug use and the way he would verbally abuse Diane when I wasn't around. He was also refusing to work or get a job and expected us to hand him everything.

One thing I have learned about loving your kids is that you will always love them. However, sometimes you don't like them very much. There are occasions where they seem to push your buttons. They can really try your patience to the limit sometimes. They can seem to find ways of doing things that grate on you. As a parent you want what is best for your children. You want them to have a better life for themselves than you had. It can be a love/hate relationship on occasions though. That was the way it was with Kevin. For some reason he seemed to feel that the world owed him a living. He thought we should just keep giving and giving to him and we should expect nothing in return. He even told Diane one time that because she was his mother she was responsible for taking care of him for the rest of his life.

Over the years we had tried to help him in every way we could. He started using drugs and getting into trouble at an early age. We had him in drug programs and paid for drug counseling. One program was an inpatient treatment facility that he was committed to for almost a year. That one seemed to work for a while, and then he would start hanging out with the same type of people and the same group of friends. When he did that, it would start up all over again. The fact is that you tend to become like those you are associating with. Kevin seemed to gravitate toward people who were into a lifestyle that revolved around drugs and seemed to live for the next high.

He dropped out of high school not long after he turned sixteen. He soon found out that we expected him go get a job and support himself and that he couldn't just lay around the house as he wanted to do. Kevin wound up getting his GED, and we paid to get him into trade school. He quickly found out that you actually had to work in trade school, so that didn't last long. We then paid to get him enrolled in college. We told him as long as he was in school he didn't have to pay rent. However, if he wasn't in school he was expected to get a job, pay rent, and support himself. He went to St. Petersburg College for a short time and dropped out again. We got him into several apartments and got him several jobs to get him out on his own. He always either quit or got fired and was often kicked out of the places we got him to live. I even had him work for me a couple times at the shop, but each time he refused to work and I had to fire him. He seemed to think that because he was my son, he didn't have to work while he was there. He was always shown what was expected of him, but he just refused to do it.

Naturally as parents we wanted the best for Kevin. We tried to make sure he got an education and tried everything we to make him self-sufficient and be able to support himself. We tried everything from positive reinforcement to tough love. Nothing seemed to work. He wanted to live life his way, and no one could tell him any different. We told him that he could do that on his own but not in our house. He was twenty-three by this time, and it was time for him to leave and support himself. We gave him a deadline of August 27, 2010, to be out of our house. That deadline also went for Jeremy and his family.

Diane and I were going to buy our new home and move on to the next chapter of our lives. The next chapter was one where Diane and I would finally have a place of our own and be alone together. We were so looking forward to that! The property we found in Wesley Chapel seemed to be an ideal place to make our dreams come true. We visited the area often and saw the deer and other wildlife running around the area. Diane and I both loved that. We were so excited about the thought of our new beginning. We started planning on how our new house would be. We looked at different builders and floor plans, different color schemes and tiles, etc. We planned on how the house would be set back on the property and where the pool would go. The existing house needed a couple things done before we could move in there, and then we could start construction of our dream home next door. We had begun the process of negotiating on the two properties and making an offer. It was a very exciting time for us.

The love I felt for Diane was amazing. We were more than just a husband and wife. We both felt that we had been brought together to share our lives in every way. We loved spending every moment we could with each other. She was my wife and my lover. We were also best friends and could talk about anything together, which we often did. We talked of our hopes and our dreams. We talked of our pasts and were so excited to talk of our future together. Here we were making plans for our future and about to actually witness our dreams come true! The things we talked about in the past were actually about to unfold in front of our eyes. We were going to witness our house built from the ground up with love and excitement.

In May of 2010, Diane's niece asked her if we would like to go on a cruise with them to celebrate their anniversary. She told her that she didn't think we could because we had people staying with us and probably couldn't get away. She would ask me though. When she told me about the cruise, I said, "Sure! When do we leave?"

I knew we needed a break from the conditions at home. With so many people living together in one house it can sometimes infringe on your privacy, and we were due for a vacation. This would be the perfect opportunity. The cruise that we were going on had the same itinerary as the one we took years ago when we first got engaged. What a fabulous way to recharge our batteries. We visited the jewelry store we got engaged at and stopped at Carlos and Charley's. We found that our love for each other was even deeper now, and we appreciated this opportunity to be able to express our love in the privacy of our cabin! One day at sea we never came out of our room and just enjoyed each other and the views from our balcony. Room service was our only interruption.

When we got back from our cruise, the tension between Diane and

Kevin continued to escalate. He kept wanting us to extend the move-out deadline we had given him. When we refused, he would often wait until I was out of the house and then badger Diane for an extension. This was witnessed by my son Jeremy, his family, and others many times. She had resorted to locking herself in our room just to get away from the constant bombardment of pestering and threats. He would often stand outside the door and bang on it, demanding that she let him in to talk to her. When she refused, he tried whatever he could to get in. On one occasion he had actually kicked in the door just to get to her. I then installed a deadlock on our bedroom door. Not long after that, he kicked through that as well. I wound up having to have the entire door and frame replaced.

The culmination of our dilemma finally came out on August 15, 2010. Diane was strangled to death in our bed on that Sunday afternoon. Kevin was arrested and charged with her murder. Almost two years afterward, he was convicted of Diane's death and sentenced to life in prison for it. The trial started on July 18, which was Diane's birthday. It would have been her fifty-first birthday. He was found guilty on July 24, my birthday. He was sentenced on August 2, 2012, to life in prison. A couple years later, he wound up getting a second trial based on a technicality. There is much more I could write about this.However, there has already been so much coverage of this story in the news and on TV with two docudramas and one other show that was done about it. One was done by the Discovery Channel and the other one by *Dateline*. If anyone wants more information on that aspect of this story, they should read the court transcripts and documents that are all available as public record. There were two trials and mounds of evidence collected and presented in court. There was testimony from witnesses and depositions from those who saw what took place. This book is about love and my experiences with love. Unfortunately, that also includes the incidents in my life where love is lost, and my love for Diane and our life together was drastically cut short that fateful August afternoon. It was a life and love that was taken from me *much* too soon!

The love in my heart remains though. As with Kris, my love for Diane will remain with me forever! It remains in the memories we created together and the passionate love we shared over the years. That type of love is something that never leaves you. I feel that I have been truly blessed by the deep and abiding love I have had the pleasure experiencing with both Kris and Diane. Nothing can erase the memories I have of those two lovely ladies or the love that I have right down in my very soul. Many people never get to find love—true love—in the course of a lifetime. Here I am at this point in my life, and I have experienced it twice so far. Love, when it is so deep and when it is taken away so tragically, can be the worst pain in the world. Still, even knowing how very devastating the hurt can be, I wouldn't have missed either of those loves for anything in this world.

Love—true love—is worth it!

Chapter 17

Another Chance at Love

AFTER DIANE DIED, I LOST FOCUS ON LIFE for a while. After losing her, my life didn't seem to have much meaning. I lost my will to live and really didn't care what happened to me. I started drinking heavily again after almost twenty-five years. I was still doing real estate and flipping houses, but that didn't bring the enjoyment that it used to. To be perfectly honest, I was at a point where I was pissed off with God and that as far as I was concerned, He could just take me now! I was over this life and wanted to move on and be with the ones who I loved in this world and were now in heaven. I have always heard that God has a plan for each of us, but right now I thought God's plan for me sucked! His ways are higher than our ways, though, and there are things that happen to us that we will never have an answer to this side of heaven.

About a year after Diane died, I started dating again. The loneliness was getting to me, so I tried to fill it with girls I picked up in bars. That did very little to fill the emptiness I felt inside though. Those temporary Band-Aids just didn't do the trick for me. I had experienced what it was like to have the girl of my dream's true love, and now I was just trying not to feel so totally devastated by drowning myself with alcohol and the quick thrill of meaningless sex. It wasn't working.

I tried to get my life back on track and tried to reconcile with God as well. I started going back to church and even went on a Christian dating site to try and find another good woman. That worked a little better, but I still felt a tremendous void inside. The grief I felt was overwhelming sometimes, so I continued to turn to the bottle to try to mask the pain I felt that seemed to reside in the depths of my very soul! I would pull myself together for a few months and then go off on another bender. I was on a self-destructive path, and I knew it. Still there didn't seem to be much I could do to stop it from happening or was it that I just didn't care anymore? I couldn't tell which it was, so I continued on and tried to do the best I could. I continued attending church and even reading my Bible. I continued to date women on the Christian site and met a few very nice ladies. Inevitably I would either do something stupid like staying out all night drinking or just break things off before I felt I would hurt them. I was still feeling so empty inside and nothing I did could fill the void.

After several years of going on this way, I met a nice woman on the website. Her name was Tonya, and she was new to the dating world. We chatted back and forth about our likes and dislikes and what we enjoyed doing for fun. I told her that I rode motorcycles for fun, and I wrote that it was a BLAST, all in caps like that. She had never been on a motorcycle and couldn't imagine it being that much fun. I asked her to pick her favorite restaurant and went on a date with her. On the first date, I laid it all out there to her about my first wife Kris and how she died and about Diane and the fact that she was murdered. I figured if she didn't run after hearing all that on a first date then at least she was warned! I could claim complete disclosure. Tonya didn't run. As a matter of fact, she seemed to be intrigued by the fact that I opened up that much to her on a first date. She told me later that it was the fact that I was so open and honest with her that had her wanting to get to know me better. Some of her friends told her to run and that I had too much baggage.

She said "Hey, at this age we *all* have baggage. It's just a matter of how much and if you can handle it."

We dated several more times and had a good time. I took her for her first ride, and she *loved* it! That got her hooked, both on riding and on me. We even attended church together. She came with me to my church sometimes, and I went with her to her church other times. The more time we spent together, the deeper Tonya fell for me (this is what she told me). Our dates consisted of going to restaurants, movies, motorcycle events, and rides along with various other activities. After about three months of dating, Tonya told me that she had fallen in love with me. At the time I didn't feel the same way toward her though, and I told her that. I said, "I want to be honest with you, and I can't tell you that I feel that way about you. At least I don't feel that way right now." She told me that was okay. She would be patient and give me time. She knew that she loved me though and wanted me to know it. She asked that I just be honest with her, and I assured her that I would.

I was still drinking at this time. I just wasn't drinking as much. We would go to clubs and see local bands and sometimes wind up taking a cab home because we drank too much. In December we went on a cruise for her birthday. We went to Cozumel and rented a motorcycle and rode the whole island. It was absolutely gorgeous! Cozumel is an island that is surrounded by some of the most beautiful crystal-clear water in the world. The road that goes around it is right next to the shoreline. The views that you can see are incredible. The sound of the waves crashing on the rocks and the smell of the fresh, salty air were awesome! They have two roads that run along the coast. One is for cars, and one is for bikes. The one that is for bikes runs closest to the water and has signs all along the way that show a picture of a car with a red circle around it and a line through it as if to say, "No cars." Tonya took a picture of me that I consider to be one of the greatest bike pictures ever. It shows me sitting on a Harley with a sleeveless Harley shirt on that road with a picture of a biker painted on the road itself and that sign with the car slashed through it and the crystal-clear water in the background only a few feet away. Needless to say, we had a wonderful trip.

Back at home Tonya continued to tell me that she loved me and ask me how I felt about her. I still couldn't tell her I loved her and told her so. She would just say, "Okay, I guess I just need to give you more time." We were having a good time, and I enjoyed being with her. I just didn't feel that way about her. I explained to her the fact that I really did like being with her and I did know how love felt, but I just wasn't there. She assured me that it was okay and to be honest with her. She would just have to give me more time, she said. I agreed, but I warned her that I might not ever get there and love her like she loved me. She said she was willing to take that chance. She knew how she felt about me and that she had never felt so in love with anyone before as she was with me.

That went on for about a year with her telling me how she felt and me telling her I wasn't there yet and I needed more time. Then she told me one evening that she didn't know how much more time she could give me. She wanted the whole package and wanted me to love her too. I told her that I wished I could but that I had to be honest with her and wasn't there and might never be.

She said, "Okay, I'll give you another month."

Another month came and went, and I had the same answer for her. She told me she would give me another month. That month came and went, and still I had the same answer. She kinda got upset, and she said she was breaking up with me. She said she didn't want to live the rest of her life as just somebody's girlfriend. I agreed and told her maybe it was best for us to take a break. That lasted for less than a week, and she was back and wanting to give me more time. She told me again how she felt and said that the Bible says that love is patient and kind.

She said, "I choose love."

We continued on this way for another couple months, and she came to me again and said she wanted to know how I felt. This time I had it all set in my head what I was going to say to her. I was going to tell her to just move on. I didn't need any more time, and I didn't think I would ever love her the way she loved me. I was going to tell her that I didn't want to string her along and that she should find someone else. That is what I had planned to say.

When the time came and she asked me, what came out of my mouth was, "Please, Tonya, can you just give me a little more time?"

Where did that come from? That is exactly what I said to myself. I even looked around to see who'd said it. I couldn't believe that had just come out of my mouth! That was *not* what I planned to say at all. Naturally she said she would give me more time, and I didn't let on what I was actually thinking to myself.

God knows what He is doing. He knew that Tonya was exactly who I needed even if I didn't yet. He knew that I was what she needed too. There are no mistakes with God. The fact that those words came out of my mouth when I had an entirely different scenario all planned out in my head is evidence of that. We had been attending church more regularly and drinking way less. I had been reading my Bible more and praying again, and God heard me (actually it was probably Tonya's prayers being heard at that time). The love Tonya felt for me started growing in my heart as well, and I started to fall for her. Less than a month later, those words that she had been waiting so long to hear came out of my mouth, and I told her that I loved her. That made her the happiest woman in the world. We started growing closer and more in love. She was absolutely glowing with love, and I heard from her friends and family members how different she was with me and how happy she was. They had never seen her in love like this. The feeling had become mutual.

God had been a big part of both of our lives over the years, and both of us at one time or another had fallen away from following Him. That began to change. Tonya had turned back to him several years before we met, and I had turned back to Him after Tonya and I started going to her church, which was Calvary Baptist Church in Clearwater. We were attending church every Sunday, and we were also volunteering at the church's food pantry and had begun helping with the pack a sack program that our church has for kids who need lunch on the weekends. We would pack a sack of food and healthier snacks for them to take home. Our church also started a satellite campus for a college certificate for Christian ministry. I enrolled in the first class. We also began living together and growing closer. Our love was growing for each other, and we were very happy. We even had our families over together for Thanksgiving. Tonya loved that. She loved putting on dinner parties and decorating. I told her she could decorate, and I would cook. She agreed.

I knew after that I wanted to marry Tonya. I got a ring and planned the evening. I made reservations at our favorite restaurant, which was Charley's in Tampa. I even got our favorite table by the fish tank. After dinner was over, I ordered desert, something we rarely did, and then I pulled out the ring, got down on one knee at the table, and said "Tonya, will you marry me?"

She couldn't believe it! She smiled so big and said, "Oh my God, *yes*, yes I'll marry you!"

I then had the waiter take our picture to capture the moment forever. We left the restaurant and drove to downtown St. Pete, where I had arranged for us to take a horse and carriage ride along the waterfront. Tonya was all smiles that evening, and she looked so pretty. It was the perfect ending for a perfect night.

After that Tonya started planning the wedding. She asked what I wanted for the wedding, and I told her that all I wanted was her and that I would be just as happy getting married in the preacher's office and going on the honeymoon. Tonya wanted a big wedding though, and I agreed to let her have what she wanted. After all, you know the saying, "Happy wife, happy life." We met with a wedding planner and looked at a couple of venues. She looked at several dresses, and she took her niece to cake tastings. We contacted a local band that we liked and were going to book them to play at the wedding. My favorite band is Lynyrd Skynyrd, and Tonya thought she would surprise me by having them do our big day. She contacted them to see what it would take for them to play at the wedding. That plan was scrubbed when she found out it would cost at least $250,000 if they could do it between dates they had already booked. We (she—at this point I was just along for the ride) had picked a date in October and decided on the Don Cesar resort as the venue. We went to the jeweler and picked out our rings. There were a lot of other pretty things she wanted there, but we settled on the rings.

We contacted one of the pastors of our church and began taking marriage classes. That is something they require for anyone to be married at the church. They want to make sure that a couple is compatible and knows exactly what they are committing to. We took the preliminary test to see how compatible we were with each other and set up a meeting with him the following week. He was actually impressed with how our tests turned out and how close we answered the questions about each other. He had us each tell him basically our life story, and then he would counsel us. When he heard the part about us living together, he had to tell us what the Bible has to say about that. He told us that he wasn't condemning or judging us; that was just what God had to say in His word about our situation. We were, after all, seeking biblical counseling, and we were wanting to live the Christian life and be closer to God.

Tonya asked me what I thought, and I told her, "I told you, baby, all I wanted was to marry you. The rest is on you."

I told her she could wait until October (it was February) and have the big wedding or she could have diamonds, get married in the pastor's office, and take a trip to Hawaii. We already had our rings. She chose diamonds and Hawaii (smart lady). Two days later on February 11, 2016, we went into the pastor's office and got married in the sight of God and our pastor.

After what I had been through with first Kris dying and then Diane being taken away, my love for Tonya was what I needed at the time. God knew that. Tonya was exactly the right person for God to bring into my life. I was also exactly what she needed. We complemented each other very well. I got to show her what true love was. She told me that she had never really experienced that before. She was the one God brought into my life and helped to heal my heart and allow me to love again. It all started because we were open to love, and we were each seeking someone at the time. When love comes, you have to be open to the wonderful possibilities that love brings.

Love conquers all!

Chapter 18

Another Love Gone Too Soon

TONYA WAS A BREAST CANCER SURVIVOR. Before we met, she had gone through years of treatment for stage 4 breast cancer. She had radiation, chemotherapy, and a right breast mastectomy. When we met, she was in the maintenance phase of her treatments. I would go with her to her appointments, which she had every four months. She used to be very apprehensive about me going because those were not good days for her. Her mood would be down, and she got very upset every time she went. However, after a couple times of me going with her, she appreciated me being there and my optimism about the outcome of the visit. We began to make those doctor visits our date days and make the day fun. Sometimes we would plan a whole weekend event around it, and they became a day she would look forward to instead of dreading them as she had in the past.

She told me of a time when she was in Ohio getting treatments a few years earlier where her aunt prayed for her and she felt she was healed.

I said, "Well, if you felt healed then God healed you. The cancer is no longer in your body, and that is what I choose to believe."

I always tried to put a positive light on it and make her feel loved through it all. She said she also believed that, but she was still scared. After all, the cancer almost killed her just a few years before. The chemo and radiation had brought her to death's door, and she told me sometimes she felt as if she wouldn't survive the treatments. Her doctor told her that if she survived the treatments, she had a good chance of beating it completely.

We prayed each time before we went, and each time the report would be a little better. The spots on her chest wall were dissipating, and the injections she was getting were working. After a few visits the doctor changed the treatment to just taking a pill, and she no longer had to have the injection. Tonya was thrilled at that. The injections would wipe her out about a day and a half after she got them, and she would feel exhausted for a couple days. With the pills there were no side effects, at least none that Tonya felt.

After we were married, the cancer was in remission, and she was feeling great. We began our life together and did quite a bit of traveling. We took a few more cruises, and we went to several NASCAR races in other states. We also traveled to visit some of her relatives in Ohio and West Virginia. On those trips, we also tried to go through as many states as possible and see as much of this beautiful country as we could. Seeing God's creation all around us is one of the many blessings that we tried to make sure we enjoyed along the way. From the Smokey Mountains to the Atlantic Ocean to the Caribbean Sea, we soaked it all in and relished in every moment of it.

We had both been through quite a bit in our pasts and faced the realization of how fragile the human body can be. We both knew how precious life was and what a gift each day is. The fact was that God had given each of us a new lease on life, so we tried to make each day count and not take anything for granted. We both felt very blessed that God had brought us together, and the love we shared was amazing. At that stage of our lives, to find true love again was an unexpected pleasure and a real sign of God's grace. I honestly wondered if I ever would experience true love again. I did.

In April of 2016, Tonya and I went to her regular doctor's appointment. She wanted to have reconstructive surgery to restore her breasts after the mastectomy. Each time before the doctor was hesitant and said she could have it but thought that she should wait a while longer for everything to be cleared up on her chest wall. We agreed and said we wanted to make sure and wait until the time was right. On this visit the doctor said two magic words, words that Tonya had been waiting to hear for thirteen years. The doctor told her that she was "cancer free" and could make plans for the reconstructive surgery. We were overjoyed and thanked God for the great news! Her oncologist told her that she didn't need any more treatments and all she would need to do was to make annual visits for a checkup. She wouldn't need to come back to see her until May of 2017. Tonya contacted the plastic surgeon and started making plans to have the surgery done. By the end of May, everything was in place and she had the procedure done. Tonya went through a very long and extensive operation and about a month of recovery to have her breasts redone. She then had to have another operation in October to complete the process. With the surgery behind us, we were now ready to move on with the rest of our lives together and do things that we had always wanted to do.

Both Tonya and I loved doing charity work and volunteering at the church. One of the things I had always wanted to do was to start a nonprofit organization to help those who are in need anywhere I saw an opportunity to do so. My family and I had been helped in years past, and I wanted to pay it back and then start paying it forward. The idea was to just help people wherever I saw a need without the red tape of some other organizations and get folks the help they needed immediately. I had given Thanksgiving dinners to people who needed them over the years, helped families that were having a hard time at

Christmas, and I had started passing out roses to people in nursing homes on Valentine's Day.

Tonya said, "So what's stopping you? Let's just research how to do it and start our own nonprofit." What a novel idea! So we did.

Tonya, being the Google queen that she was, did all the research and found out what needed to be done. I contacted my attorney and had him draw up the corporate papers and register us with the state of Florida. After that we got our accountant to file the proper paperwork with the IRS. Six months later KG True North was born. KG was for my last name, Kyne, and her last name, Grass. True North is for God being our true north and guiding influence. We are a Christian-based nonprofit, and our mission is to help and guide those in need as God leads us.

Our first official event as a nonprofit was to help with the Tim Tebow Foundation and Calvary Church to put on his Night to Shine event in Clearwater. This is something Tim Tebow started a couple years ago to give special needs teens and adults a complete prom experience with tuxes and dresses, hair and makeup, limo rides, a red carpet entrance with a cheering section and paparazzi, a decked-out dance hall with DJ music, and catering. It had everything you would expect for an elaborate prom event and then some. It was a wonderful experience, and I think we got as much out of being a part of it as the attendees did, if not more. It was a truly magical evening to see the pure joy on the faces of those special individuals. It was their night to shine!

Our church was also involved in a campaign to help plant churches around the country and around the world. We had pledged to help however we could. We traveled to Pittsburgh, where our church was looking into planting a church. With my background in real estate, I thought we could help with housing for the team that was going to be there. That didn't work out, but Tonya and I got to travel more and spend more time together on the road, which was something we loved to do. We then went to Denver where our church was looking to help with a start-up church plant there. This time everything seemed to be working out just right, and God was opening doors for us. We wound up moving out there with the expectation to help with the opening of The Heights Denver.

In the process of getting ready to move out to Colorado, we made five trips back and forth from Florida to Denver. On the first two trips we made, we flew into Denver and rented a car, staying in hotels while we were there. Each time we went, Tonya felt ill for a little while after we got there. We stayed about a week each time and then returned to Florida, and about a week later Tonya would be feeling fine. Being the Google queen she was and a nurse herself for twenty years, she researched her symptoms and came up with a diagnosis of altitude sickness. Her symptoms were shortness of breath and fatigue after any exertion and an occasional headache along with it. She would also get sharp pains between her shoulder blades that would move to different places. She said it felt like air being trappedin there, and if she could just get out one big bur it would be fine. From what she read, all the evidence pointed to the altitude in Denver being the problem, and the only thing that would make things better was to stay out there for an extended period of time and let her body adjust. The problem was we didn't have a place to stay there yet. We were making plans and looking for a house to buy. We looked at several properties and put in offers, but none of the deals went through. After a few months doing this, we decided that we would rent a house, move out there, and then begin the search again.

We had prayed about this move for some time. We wanted to make sure this is the move we should be making. I told God, "Okay, God, if You want us to move out there, You are going to have to help us sell our house and find us a place in Denver so we can make this move." We put our home on the market for sale at 11 a.m. Saturday morning. That afternoon we sold our house for full asking price. The house was only on the market for six hours. After that we found a nice home just north of Denver that we were able to assume a lease on and would only have to be there for five months. That would give us time to find a place and move. We also had the option of extending the lease another year if we needed to. God was opening doors and answering prayers. We packed up our home and moved west.

Colorado is beautiful, and we enjoyed the scenery with the snow-capped mountains in the background. We got a chance to explore quite a lot of the area, from Colorado Springs all the way up to Fort Collins. The Denver area is really growing in leaps and bounds. There is a lot of construction and expansion going on. The traffic can be hectic in some areas. However, we found that there are alternate routes to get you where you need to go once you know the shortcuts and back roads. We loved exploring the area and wound up finding all kinds of restaurants, shops and other places that even those who had been there for years didn't know about. There is such an eclectic mix in the Denver area that you can find great restaurants from most ethnic groups represented. We found everything from great steaks at Buckhorn Exchange to Mexican, Jamaican, Thai, Indian, Ethiopian, Cajun, and so much more. From Denver Biscuits to Voodoo Doughnuts, it was a wonderful culinary experience.

During this time, Tonya and I were growing even closer together, and our love for one another was expanding more each day. We didn't think that was possible, but it was true. It seemed like the more time we spent together, the closer we became. We didn't only love each other; we actually liked one another too and were best friends. With all the traveling back and forth across the country and all the exploring we did in Colorado, we were together most of the time, and we really enjoyed each other's company. I felt that with Kris, I felt it with Diane, and now I had the pleasure of feeling it again with Tonya.

After we had been in Colorado for a while, Tonya began to feel worse and not better as she thought she would. Her fatigue seemed to increase and last longer, and her headaches were more frequent. The pain between her shoulder blades was still there, and now it was sometimes moving into her ribs. She contacted several medical professionals that she knew and asked their opinions on her condition. She was convinced that it was caused by altitude sickness and she just needed more time to adjust to the climate and elevation we were at. In Florida we lived near the coast and everything was close to sea level. Now here we were in Denver at an elevation of over five thousand feet. According to the people she talked to and the research she did online, her symptoms indicated that the altitude was the culprit, and nothing but time and rest would alleviate the problem. I wasn't convinced of that and wanted her to get to the hospital and get a thorough examination. She refused to go though, and she could be quite stubborn about it.

This went on for a couple more weeks, and I finally told her "Look, you are getting worse and not better. If it was altitude sickness, it should have subsided by now. I'm taking you to the hospital."

Tonya refused and told me that if I made her go as I said I would, she would jump out of the car when I came to a stop. She was not waiting in any emergency room while they ran tests and couldn't find anything. She felt she was a medical professional and knew her body better than anyone else. She had her yearly checkup scheduled at Moffitt Cancer Center in Florida next month and she was going to wait until then. I finally relented and agreed to postpone a trip to the hospital for now.

I had gone to work for Jiffy Lube in Colorado as a manager and trainer for their mechanics as they were expanding their business to include a full line of automotive repair. I had only been there a week when Tonya became worse a couple days later and I gave the company a week's notice and told them the situation. We were going back to Florida and getting her evaluated for what was going on. We called Moffitt and got her appointment moved up a couple weeks and planned to leave the following Monday. Friday when I came in from work, Tonya was feeling badly and said she was worried. Her symptoms now included being a little dizzy and occasional blurred vision. I quickly tossed some stuff in suitcases and told her we were leaving that night. I wasn't waiting any longer. She agreed, and we loaded up the car and started out for Florida. At this point Tonya was still convinced it was altitude sickness and that her body was just not adjusting. I believed that something else was going on. I didn't know what it was, and I didn't have the medical background she did, but I knew that it was more serious than what she thought it was.

On our way back across the country, we could only drive for a few hours at a time. Tonya would have to stop and couldn't endure riding in the car for very long. She also felt that she wouldn't be able to get through an airport and be confined sitting inside of a plane for hours either. I had suggested that before we left Denver and thought it would be best to fly and get her checked out sooner. The trip usually takes a few days to drive back. This trip was taking over a week. We got as far as north Florida, and Tonya felt as if she couldn't go any farther. She needed to be checked out immediately. We found the Mayo Clinic in Jacksonville, and I took her into the ER.

The attending physician listened to Tonya explain her symptoms and what she had been experiencing. She told him about the things she had researched and how she thought it was altitude sickness. She explained to him the way she was short of breath and the fatigue that set in and how it was getting worse. The dizziness and blurred vision were making it hard to be in bright lights. She was also having pain between her shoulder blades and in her ribs sometimes. The pain would move from place to place, and she said it felt like air was trapped in her body that had no way of escaping. That was one of the reasons she thought it was altitude sickness. Tonya also told him of her history with cancer and how we were headed back to Moffitt for her annual checkup. He then ordered a series of tests and a complete blood work on her. He said that he would wait for the test results and get back with us.

When the first results came back from the blood work and scans, the doctor came in and told us that he didn't see anything abnormal about the results. He said he would be back after the other tests came back. Tonya began to be worried.

She said, "You see, this is why I didn't want to go to the hospital. They are not going to find anything wrong, and they are not going to believe me and just send me home!" She began to cry, so I tried to assure her that I was not going to let her leave that hospital without finding out what was wrong. I began to pray and ask God to let the doctor believe Tonya and run all the tests necessary to find the cause of her symptoms and get to the bottom of this.

The doctor came back a little while later and said that the results of all the tests had come back and didn't show anything at all. There was a bit of an abnormality in some of the blood work but nothing that would explain any of her symptoms. I told him that there had to be something they could do and some other tests they could run to figure this out.

Tonya said, "You see, I told you he wouldn't believe me."

The doctor said that he did believe her and she didn't seem like the type of person who would make up something like that. They did see patients come into the hospital that did make stuff up, but Tonya was not one of those, he said. The doctor told us that with her history, there were a few more tests he could run that might give an explanation about her condition, so he ordered the tests. He would be back to talk with us when the tests came back.

After about an hour, he came back and said, "I think I have some bad news for you. I am not an expert in this area, but we found some areas around your rib cage and in your skull that don't look good. I think your cancer has returned. We want to admit you and let the oncology team assess the situation."

They called upstairs and got a room ready and transferred us up to the cancer floor of the main hospital. The next day we met with the oncology team and went over the results and they ran a few more tests. What they found out was that the cancer had not only returned but had come back with a vengeance and spread everywhere. It was in her rib cage and in her skull and in her liver and other organs. The prognosis was not good. They told us that with treatment she may have up to a few months to live and without treatment maybe a few weeks at the most.

Our first reaction was shock and devastation. At first we couldn't believe it. This was not something we ever thought would happen. Tonya knew how bad the treatments were, and she didn't want to have to go through them again. Just a year ago she was given a clean bill of health and told she was cancer free. Even after all the reconstructive surgery, there was no indication anything was wrong. Her last checkup after the surgery was in late November. This was only six months later. How could the cancer have come back so quickly and spread so extensively in only that short a period of time. I held Tonya in my arms, and we wept together bitterly for a while.

When you get news like this, what do you do? There was nothing we could do to keep it from happening. We had prayed about it, and we were praying for a miracle. After all, we had seen miracles happen before. We also knew that we had to surrender to what God wanted, and we prayed that His will be done. The worst that could happen, after all, was that Tonya would get to go to heaven a little sooner than we thought. We could either bitch and moan about it or we could choose to look at it that way and have a positive attitude and enjoy the time we had left together. We chose to be positive and enjoy the time we had left with each other. The smile came back to our faces, and we told them that even with this prognosis no one could threaten us with heaven!

After a few days in the hospital, they stabilized Tonya, and we came back to the Tampa Bay area. We got a house close to her mother and brother, and we got her back to Moffitt Cancer Center. They confirmed what the Mayo Clinic had said. They did a round of radiation treatment on her head to reduce the impact of the tumors pressing on her optic nerve. They said that was what was causing her dizziness and headaches and made her sensitive to light. After that they would see where we were and recommend a course of action.

I had to leave Tonya in the capable hands of her mother and brother while I flew back out to Denver to pack up our house and bring our furniture and things back to Florida. I didn't want to leave her, but I knew it had to be done. At least we had that short-term lease and didn't have to worry about having two places to pay for. The process should have taken about ten days or so. I was back in six days, including driving across country with the truck towing my motorcycle and trailer loaded down with stuff.

When I got back, we moved into a place that Tonya picked out. I got everything moved in while she was staying at her brother's house. He was such a blessing to us and opened up his home for us to stay with him while we were in this transition period. We talked about our feelings and what was coming. She wasn't afraid to die. She was just sorry that she had to go first and that I would be left here to mourn another wife. She didn't want me to be sad, and she wanted me to go out and find love again. We spent as much time together as possible, and we made trips out to the Courtney Campbell Causeway, where Tonya would just sit and look at the water. That was the place she fell in love with Florida when she first came down from Ohio many years earlier.

We went back to Moffitt, and they told us the cancer was spreading even more aggressively than they had first thought. There was nothing they could do to prevent the inevitable from happening. She could either stay there in the hospital or go to Hospice. Tonya decided she wanted to go home, so that's what we did. We set up hospice to come to the house, and her brother and I brought her home. Shortly after that on July 22, 2017, Tonya Lynn Grass went to be with the Lord. It was just six weeks from the time she was diagnosed at the Mayo Clinic that she passed away. This time I got to be there with my wife in her last moments. I got to let her know at that moment how much I loved her. I was holding her in my arms when she left this earth.

Love taken too soon, again.

Chapter 19

The Rest of the Story

WHAT IS THE REST OF THE STORY? ACTUALLY, I'm not sure. It hasn't been written yet. Sitting down and writing this book has been a unique experience for me. If I didn't live all of this, I would think that this is a story someone had made up. It could have been written for a novel or a movie or some other work of fiction. I know better though. I was there, and I experienced all of this and more. They say that sometimes fact is stranger than fiction. I'm not sure who "they" are, but it's true in this case. My life has taken many unusual twists and turns. However, the one constant in it has been *love*. I couldn't have made it this far without it.

Love has many different forms and is used in many different ways to express our feelings for someone or something important in our lives. There can be the love between a father and a son or daughter or between a mother and her child. There is the love you have for your brothers and sisters. The love between special friends can be an incredible bond. You can have a love for many other people in your life, like a student or a teacher, a boss or coworker or a doctor or other professional that you feel this way toward. I'm talking about a healthy kind of love though and not some of the sick and twisted things that seem to be permeating our society these days.

Love can also be used to describe how we feel about certain things as well. Some of us love our cars, some people love their boats, or in my case, I love my motorcycle. You can love your home or your job or your Bose surround sound system with the Sony eighty-inch HDTV that you use to watch all your sporting events and movies that you also love. You can say you love Chicago deep-dish pizza or German chocolate cake, or in Tonya's case she loved Voodoo doughnuts. Diane loved Charley's Steakhouse filet mignon. Kris loved Alaskan king crab. Toby Keith even wrote a song saying, "I love this bar." Yes, there are many different ways that we express love.

The love between a man and a woman is one of my favorite kinds of love, though. It can take you to such highs in your life, and the loss of it can bring you to the deepest lows as well. That has been my experience with this crazy thing called love. I wouldn't have missed any of it for the world though. As Garth Brooks wrote in his song called, "The Dance," "I could have missed the pain, but I'd have had to miss the dance." The dance is the juice of life between a man and a woman to me. The pain you may have to go through is worth it, or at least it has been for me. I have had the distinct pleasure of spending almost thirty-seven years of my life with three absolutely amazing women. Each one was an exciting experience all on their own. All three had their own unique way of loving me that only they could do. Each one was so passionate and awesome that I would never want to have missed any of it. I will carry each one with me in my heart, in my mind, and in my very soul as long as I live. I thank God for each of them. All three made me a better man in their own way, and each one was exactly what I needed at that time in my life.

My life has been quite an adventure so far. I feel like I have a lot more living to do. It is almost as if I have lived four separate and complete lives up to this point. The life I lived up until the time I met Kris seemed like a completely different life than the one I lived after we met and started raising a family. Once I met and fell in love with Diane, it seemed like another complete lifetime. The time we spent together and the things we did were amazing. After Diane was taken, I never for an instant thought it could happen again—love, that is. Then Tonya came along and helped heal my heart, and I was able to love again. The time Tonya and I spent together wasn't that long in years, but we packed a lot of living and loving into those few years. I choose to remember all the good times I had with each of those fabulous ladies. That is what helps keep me going. The memories of life and love that lasts a lifetime are so precious to me. Each love with my wives was distinct. Each had their own special moments, and each will last a lifetime in my mind and in my heart.

Where will you find your love? Have you found your true love yet? Is it really out there for you? If you have found your love, please don't take it for granted. This life can be very short, and you never know what tomorrow may bring. We are not even guaranteed that we will have a tomorrow. Let that special someone know how you feel. Show them with flowers or a card or a little gift for no reason other than because you were thinking of them. Tell them how you feel and just say, "Baby, I love you" out of the blue. Hold hands with them when you are walking down the street. A little kiss when you come home can make a world of difference to that special someone in your life. If that's not a normal thing for you, *make* it a normal thing! This life is meant to be lived, and as Tony Robbins says, "Live your life with *passion!*" It's so much more fun and rewarding when you do.

There is another kind of love that you don't want to ignore, and that's God's love. It can be and should be the most important love of all. No matter who or where you are, God loves you. He loves us so much that He sent His only Son to die on a cross to take away our sin so we can have a relationship with Him. All you have to do is accept His free gift of salvation for you. Jesus Christ was sent to earth to die for the sins all humankind has committed, and He was raised the third day to conquer death so that we can have eternal life if we believe that in our hearts. Like love, it is a heart thing and a belief. Please go and read a few verses and let God speak to you. One is a verse most people know: John 3:16. The other is also pretty widely known, and that is Romans 10:9–10. There are plenty more passages and a lot more verses that could be quoted. However, this gives you a great start. God's love is amazing, and I felt compelled to include it in this book. My life and this book would be nowhere without God's love.

Well, this is about the end of this book. What is the rest of the story? Will I find love again? Only time will tell. I will say one thing, though. I will be open to all the possibilities. I will remain on the lookout for it. Will it come to me again? I certainly hope so. Love—*true* love—is worth it! Only *true* love can take you to the pinnacle of the highest mountaintop of emotion with no fear and complete and utter joy! The special love and bond between a man and a woman who find *true* love for one another is the most fabulous feeling in the world! My hope and prayer for everyone who reads this book is that you find your own *truelove!*

Love truly can last a lifetime!

Printed in the United States
By Bookmasters